INTEGRATED TREATMENT FOR CO-OCCURRING DISORDERS

For My Father

Contents

CONTENTS

Acknowledgments

Thanks and feelings of gratitude to my Wiley editors, Marquita Flemming and Sherry Wasserman. Thank you for the support and kind words during this project. I am indebted to Ken Minkoff, MD, and Donald Meichenbaum, PhD, for their insights on co-occurring disorders, and to my wife, Rebecca Klott, PhD, for her continued guidance, support, and encouragement.

CHAPTER ONE

Introduction

An Examination of the Guiding Principles for Treating Co-Occurring Disorders

I would like to begin this book with a story. The story is about one of the more important events—and lessons—in my 45-year career as an addiction counselor. At the time, I had been in the profession for 10 years. Most of my efforts with clients resulted in extreme frustration. My practice was marked by noncompliance, relapse, recidivism, confrontation, and, basically, poor outcomes. My clients were getting nothing from me, and I was becoming a poster child for burnout. Perhaps some of you have been to this place. I remember dreaming about working in a flower shop or, my favorite escape fantasy, in a bookstore. During this time I placed the blame for my inadequate results on the clients. After all, I would proclaim to myself, I am appropriately applying the skills that I was taught in my graduate program that would enable these people to surrender the plague of drugs and alcohol from their lives. The problem, therefore, could not possibly be with me. The problem was with the clients and the fact that they were "just not ready." I am sure that many of you have heard the old mantra in drug counseling that "addicts have to

1

hit rock bottom" before they see their behaviors as problematic. I would do my best to point out to them that their use of drugs and/or alcohol was destroying both themselves and those around them. They would not listen. I would educate them about the effects of drugs and alcohol on their brains and other body functions. They would not listen. I would resort, at times, to emotional blackmail. They would leave counseling. I was not a good counselor.

It was at this point that I was invited to participate in a two-week seminar sponsored by the Veteran's Administration. The seminar was designed to acquaint us with a new treatment strategy for addiction disorders — Motivational Enhancement Therapy. This strategy, which is discussed at length in Chapter 5, had some glowing research outcomes. I was excited. I knew I could benefit from anything that would help change what I was doing. This training resulted in the watershed event of my career, but it began as a very humbling experience.

Three days into this training, I was gently confronted by one of the presenters regarding my attitude toward the skills being taught. These skills appeared, in my humble estimate, to be enabling. I was also presenting myself as being confused. This was a very appropriate observation because I was, indeed, confused. I was being presented with material that went against most of what I was taught regarding the treatment of addiction disorders. My "slap-face" methods were being attacked, and being put on the defensive did not sit well with me. At any rate, this wonderful gentleman comes to me and says: "Jack, your problem is that you are an addiction counselor." I responded that this was a marvelous observation. He looked at me and respectfully replied: "Jack, hopefully, what you will learn from us is that we don't treat addictions; we treat people with addictions." He was telling me that I was locked into my professional definition. I am sure that those reading this book are very aware and sensitive to this frame of treating people and not behaviors. We don't treat addicts. We don't treat alcoholics. We treat people with addiction disorders. We do not define our clients by their DSM diagnosis! These are conditions our clients have, and these conditions do not define people. All of you are aware of this. Sadly, at this time in my career, I was not. I defined myself as an addictions counselor so, therefore, I treated addictions. This was my problem.

I also discovered I had another problem. This person would not leave me alone. He made me his project. Why? To this day I have no answer for this. What I can tell you is he saved my career and, in doing so, helped me help others. He also helped me understand myself and why I became an addiction counselor. This lesson was perhaps the most profound, sobering, and centering message and will be discussed at a later time. He also informed me that people use, abuse, and depend on drugs for a reason. In their view there is a benefit to this behavior. It is essential, he says to me, that we are empathic to this situation. When we look at all dysfunctional, maladaptive, or pathologic behaviors, we will discover that folks engage in these behaviors for a reason. All behaviors are purposeful. One of the goals in counseling is helping the client discover what that benefit or goal is.

Edwin Shneidman and Marsha Linehan, in the realm of suicide, tell us that these behaviors are either *operant* or *respondent*. In the respondent frame, we would look at drug or alcohol use as a behavior designed to achieve some control in a threatening situation or stimulus event (Linehan, 1999). An example would be the case of an individual described by others as "shy to a fault." In reality he or she is experiencing an undetected, untreated social phobia. As the person is presented with the challenging task of a coerced social interaction, he or she uses drugs or alcohol to diminish fear and have a relatively enjoyable social contact. Another case would be the person with psychotic episodes who discovers in cannabis use a calming of those intrusive episodes.

In the operant frame, Linehan tells us that drug use is elicited by a need for people to affect their environment (Linehan, 1999). Operant behaviors are those that are under the control of the consequences. An example is the often-used frame of "bonding with Budweiser." This would be individuals who continue to use drugs to maintain friendships, and they fear that sobriety and abstinence would result in the loss of those friendships. As we get to know these people, we explore their history of drug and/or alcohol use. We discover with them the operant and/or respondent benefits of their use. We may find they are the self-medicating mentally ill, or they are alone, or they need to escape a terrible reality, or they need to enhance a boring existence, or they need to avoid horrible withdrawal symptoms. Whatever the benefit may be, it is critical that we and the clients discover that benefit.

My presenter, and soon-to-be close friend, told me that in his entire career he never met a person who had the goal—as they began their history of drug or alcohol use—to become addicted. The physical, emotional, psychological addiction to their drug was the terrible consequence of a behavior that had, at the time, a very attractive motivation. The essential question during any evaluation is "What does the drug do for you?"

Regarding the self-medicating mentally ill—people with co-occurring drug/alcohol and mental disorders—Ken Minkoff tells us: "People with serious mental illnesses are vulnerable to substance use because the substance replaces prescribed psychotropic medication in order to bring relief from acute symptoms, remedy feelings of social isolation, and creates a temporary sense of well being" (Minkoff & Regner, 1999). I remember talking to a client who had a significant psychotic condition. We discovered that his cannabis use was designed to gain some relief from his symptoms. As we inched toward encouraging him to give a prescribed medication a chance to do the same thing and achieve the same goal, he says to me: "Well, tell me, can I party on these meds? And will my friends do the meds with me? And can it give me the same mellow feeling that weed does?" Substance use often begins as a "treatment" for an undiagnosed, untreated mental illness. This use evolves to become a persistent management strategy for stressors and the symptoms of the mental illness. Then, depending on multiple factors, the use becomes an addiction.

For a definition and conceptualization of co-occurring disorders, luminaries such as Ken Minkoff and Donald Meichenbaum offer us the following thoughts, which I will, respectfully, summarize. One disorder may, for instance, regularly precede the development of the other disorder. Therefore, the first disorder may be viewed as a significant risk factor or precipitant for the second (co-occurring)

4

disorder. A common example is seen in people with an undiagnosed, untreated Generalized Anxiety Disorder. This condition, which possibly emerged during late childhood or early adolescence, may render the individual vulnerable to the use of cannabis for the purpose of transient, temporary symptom relief. Research cited by Meichenbaum states that for individuals with co-occurring psychiatric and substance-related disorders, the mental health disorders usually precede the substance use disorder about 90% of the time. The median onset age of the psychiatric disorder is 11, with the substance-related disorder usually developing 5 to 10 years after the psychiatric disorder (median age of 21). Many cannabis users have told me: "When I'm stoned, I don't have a worry in the world. My life is intolerable without weed." It is not a stretch to conceptualize mental disorders as risk factors and precipitating conditions for the development of substance use disorders.

Another concept is that one disorder may act as a protective factor to another (co-occurring) disorder. When a client tells me that alcohol use allows her to "see another day," I respect that alcohol use helps her manage the unbearable grief of losing a husband and, actually, protects her from dying by suicide. It is, therefore, not a stretch to view alcohol/drug use, in some circumstances, as keeping a person from acting on suicidal impulses. A young woman in her thirties with significant issues of posttraumatic stress disorder (PTSD) resulting from a history of ritual sexual assault as a child is now heavily addicted to prescription drugs to help her sleep and, according to her, "so I won't jump off a bridge."

A final view of co-occurring disorders is when one disorder modifies and/or complicates the presentation of another (co-occurring) disorder. Addiction is a brain disease, and it is chronic. We will discuss the importance of the chronic nature of addictions at a later point in this book. Many of the problematic behaviors we see in people who use drugs are a result of brain dysfunctions. We observe in the process of the DSM, when the issue of substance-induced disorder is examined, that we are urged to diagnose carefully, cautiously, methodically, slowly. We want to differentiate between an individual with schizophrenia and the person with a substance-induced psychotic disorder. We will approach, and treat, the person with dysthymia in a different fashion than the individual with a substance-induced mood disorder. The concern for the co-occurring self-medicating mentally ill person is that the drug that provides them with transient relief from their symptoms could, in a matter of degrees, make their condition more complex. Neuroscience has uncovered how addiction to drugs hijacks different parts of the brain. The chemical dopamine conditions the brain to certain behaviors that are correlated to pleasure. Therefore, while the drug use is designed for symptom relief, the dopamine reaction creates a physiologic and emotional dependency. It is in the dependency and the continued use of the drug that will distort, modify, alter, and complicate symptomatic presentation.

PURPOSEFUL BEHAVIOR

All behaviors are purposeful. This cycle presents clinicians with, perhaps, their most significant challenge. I remember a client who once proclaimed to me during our first session together: "Telling me to quit my cocaine is like telling me to quit breathing." For that client, drug use had become an essential part of his existence. The use of drugs had a varied purpose: To assist in the management of the intrusive symptoms of his mental illness, to present him with opportunities for social interaction, and to avoid the terrible reactions of withdrawal created by the dopamine-induced dependency. This person, and many like him, presented a unique challenge in therapy. Treatment effectiveness studies on this matter are quite clear and discouraging: "Non compliance with treatment, recidivism, and multiple relapses in the substance use disorder population have been directly linked to a co-occurring mental illness" (Minkoff, 1999). Donald Meichenbaum adds to this concern: "Relapse rates among chemical addictions (heroin, cocaine, nicotine, alcohol) and across various treatment models are fairly uniform and discouraging — around 75%. The likelihood of life-long abstinence is low" (Meichenbaum, 2010). In 2010 the National Institute on Drug Abuse estimated that in the United States there were approximately 25 million people with a definable substance use disorder. Two million—less than 10%—sought help. But there is hope. I would not be engaged in this writing project if there was no hope. I am not, by nature, a pessimistic person.

Finally, this wise man at the conference tells me: "Nobody changes behaviors without motivation." That was the purpose of the training— how to motivate our clients toward abstinence and sobriety. I thought I did that. I thought that when I outlined for them how drugs and/ or alcohol were destroying their health and educated them about the effects of drugs on their brains that this cognitive input would surely motivate them to quit. I thought that when I confronted them for hurting their family with their drug use that this emotionally charged blackmail would motivate them to quit. I thought that was motivation enough. I was wrong, and to this day I feel a certain shame about this behavior.

What, then, *does* motivate people to change behaviors? The simple answer, as William Miller and Stephen Rollnick describe it: "Intrinsic motivation for change occurs in an accepting, empathic relationship in which the person discovers that current behaviors keep them from achieving what is wanted and valued in their lives" (Miller & Rollnick, 2002). This is what is called the *discrepancy* in a person's life. The person becomes aware of the fact that "this is not the way I wanted my life to be." As we will discuss in later chapters, this focus should become the primary task of therapy. In the discovery and acknowledgment of this discrepancy, we may find the source of our client's motivation to change.

Most people who seek our help and guidance and are powerfully motivated have, on their own accord, discovered their discrepancy. They have acknowledged, in paying close attention to life's messages, that this (drug and/or alcohol use and dependency) is not the way they want life to be. They are motivated to engage, perhaps, in a brutal period of medically supervised detoxification. They are motivated to attend, for the rest of their lives, support groups. They are motivated to engage in counseling to learn and acquire new ways of coping with life's stressors and demands. They respond to counseling in a positive manner. They are motivated.

REASONS FOR SEEKING THERAPY

It has been my experience that there are basically three reasons why people seek out therapy. The first reason is that they are currently experiencing unbearable levels of emotional, psychological, and psychiatric pain. This sense of pain is a great motivator for change. This pain is individually defined by the person. Something is wrong in his or her life. Something is not the way it should be. This pain is often the discrepancy that Miller and Rollnick talk about. The most important feature here, however, is the individual nature of this pain or discrepancy. This pain has to be managed. I remember talking to a young woman who was in her second academic year at a local university. She had recently made a suicide attempt, and while she was in the emergency room, traces of alcohol and cocaine were found in her system. During our initial interview I asked her what the attempt to take her life was designed to accomplish. She looked at me and responded: "I just got my very first B." Now, that hardly seems to be a good reason to kill oneself. But for this young woman, at this period in her life, and with the individual stressors placed on her by her family for perfection, the decision to die appeared very logical to her. Her individualized definition of this failure was causing her unbearable emotional pain. She feared losing her parents' love and approval. She told me: "My parents don't accept failure." This pain defied her capacity to cope. She tried drugs, but this was not successful in curbing the pain. Finally, suicide was decided on as the ultimate problem solver.

Or consider the woman grieving the sudden loss of her husband of 38 years. To help her sleep and ease her anxiety-driven grieving, "a few" glasses of wine each night appears very appropriate—and helpful. Until, of course, this behavior for coping becomes a dependency—both physical and psychological. A wise man once told me in regards to this pain: "One person's unbearable pain is another person's irksome event." This pain is defined by the client.

Many of you have experienced this situation. When we experience intolerable levels of physical pain, we run to our primary care physician. We are diagnostically clear in indicating to that person the nature of the pain. We tell our healthcare provider everything he or she needs to know about our pain. And, most important, we respond to our physician's direction to make this pain go away. In the arena of mental health, people in this level of pain usually make for very motivated clients. They are diagnostically clear, wanting us to know as much as possible about their pain. And they will normally respond in a positive fashion to insights and directions from us that they perceive as potentially helpful in the alleviation of their pain.

Edwin Shneidman, the icon of the study of suicide in our society, told us many years ago:

> The first task of therapy is to discover the locus of the client's unbearable pain and to decrease the perturbation associated with that condition. In the context of a caring relationship we assist the person in discovering their pain and help them manage this condition. There are really only two questions we need to ask a person: "Where do you hurt?" and "how can I help you?" (Shneidman, 1973)

I am sure it comes as no surprise to many of you that a significant number of the people we have the privilege to meet are self-medicating an intolerable level of pain. That pain, again, is individually defined by the person and may vary from emotional to physical or mental. For these people, at this time in their lives, these drugs are very beneficial and attractive. Many of them, however, run a significant risk of becoming physically and/or emotionally dependent on this form of coping.

Our responsibility to these folks is to be empathic to the current purpose and benefit involved in their drug/alcohol use. Telling them to quit their drug or mandating abstinence as a contract of therapy can be damaging, harmful, and could motivate them to see therapy as "demanding too much." The practice of abstinence-mandated therapy could tragically strip them of a defense strategy that opens up significant vulnerability to suicide or other self-harm activities.

The second reason why people seek therapy is that they are being threatened with a loss of something important and meaningful to them if they do not seek counseling. Let us look at an example that many of you are familiar with: It is the person who has been told by a spouse, partner, or mate that if they don't stop drinking, they will lose that relationship. They appear in counseling with the proclamation: "My wife doesn't like my drinking. She told me that if I don't do something about it she is going to leave." And then they may add: "I need to learn to control my drinking, handle it better, become a social drinker." These people are ambivalent about abstinence and sobriety. Part of them is motivated by the threat of the loss, and part of them is reluctant to quit entirely because alcohol presents some benefits to them. These benefits could include friendships they have gained over the years at the local pub, that alcohol use calms withdrawal symptoms, or that alcohol has an effect on an undiagnosed, untreated mental illness.

What we do know is that the *only* reason these people are seeking treatment is because of the threat. Without this threat, we would never have the chance to meet them. It is essential that we accept their current ambivalence. We accept where they are at this time and place in their lives. We also respect that once that threat is gone or minimized or reduced, therapy might well be over.

There is also the possibility, slight as it may be, that they may be able to achieve the goal of being "social drinkers." We may find that in using Harm Reduction strategies, we may allow them to continue drinking while not damaging their marital relationship. We discuss these strategies in Chapter 7. Although I am not a proponent of Harm Reduction, I will engage these strategies with the ambivalent client. There are times where harm reduction is the best we can hope for with ambivalent clients. In this same chapter, we discuss how we may use Motivational Enhancement strategies to move and resolve ambivalent clients into people who are motivated to change.

The third, and final, reason why people seek out therapy is coercion. They are told to go to counseling. More often than not, this order comes from the legal system. A drug court, parole agent, or probation officer has ordered them, with dire consequences if they do not comply, to seek counseling. These people are *not* motivated, and they are *not* ambivalent; they are resistant. They would rather be anywhere other than your office. This resistance comes in many forms and presentations. Miller and Rollnick tell us that resistance is displayed by the client, basically, in four presentations. Let us briefly examine each resistance presentation.

We have, first of all, the Rationalizing client. These are people who love to argue and debate. They spend most of their time discussing with you the benefits of their behavior and the advantages of the status quo. They also love to trap the clinician in what I call the "great debate." I have had numerous encounters with these people, and I have found, to my dismay, that once they trap you in the "great debate," they will never let you go. With delight they discuss the benefits and harmless effects of cannabis. Once you step into this conversation, you will see a smile on their face. You are now theirs, and they control the counseling. You may try to extract yourself from this great debate format, but they are relentless.

Next we have the Reluctant client. These are people who fear change. They are quite accepting of the status quo, regardless of the dysfunction or pathology it may present. A request to change behaviors creates significant anxiety in them. They will often beg you to "not rock the boat" or state that "things are better off the way they are." They do not see any advantages to change and, actually, see significant disadvantages.

The third presentation is the Rebellious client, and they can be a cause for concern. These are people who learned at a very early age that hostility is a useful tool for controlling their social environment. These people are quite confrontational, and they will challenge your authority and expertise. They also, on occasion, run a risk of being physically assaultive. Their goal is to control the relationship with you by using aggressive and confrontational tactics.

And, finally, we have the Resigned client. These people present the greatest concern because of their vulnerability to suicide. They have been through the system. They have experienced multiple relapses, and you happen to be the 15th counselor they have seen for their issues. They often tell you: "I could write the book on addiction counseling. There is nothing new you can give to me.

What are you going to do any different than the other counselors I've seen?" They are hopeless and often depressed. They need very special care. We later describe these four forms of resistance in greater detail and describe appropriate counseling approaches for them.

In 1954, Harry Stack Sullivan made a comment pertaining to the newly published DSM-I. He said: "The first goal in the therapy relationship is to discover who is this person and how does this person come to be here." He was advocating, obviously, that we treat people and not diagnostic categories. He feared, as many theorists did in reaction to the *Diagnostic and Statistical Manual,* that we could reduce our clients to nothing more than a neatly arranged set of symptoms. As a result, he was concerned that clinicians would place more emphasis on those behavioral issues than on the people sitting in their offices. As it turns out, he had every right to voice that concern, but he also urged us to determine what circumstances brought the person to our services. He was acutely aware that our clients come to us under a variety of different circumstances: They are strongly motivated because of an unbearable level of emotional, mental, or physical pain; they are ambivalent about being with us; or they are in a state of resistance. Therefore, he says to us, treat the person and discover the circumstances that bring this person to your office.

Treat the person and not the diagnosis. Respect that all behaviors are purposeful. Remain mindful that nobody changes behaviors without motivation. These essential guiding principles are the framework of this book. They will be repeated quite often as we examine the challenging population of people with co-occurring disorders.

Ken Minkoff, one of the icons in the study of co-occurring disorders, examines additional guiding principles in the treatment of this condition. He tells us that an awareness of individuals with co-occurring disorders has improved and increased considerably over the last few decades. With that increase in awareness and understanding, several best practice treatment models have been developed for this population. He talks about the basic principles that support those treatment approaches.

The first, and perhaps the most important, is a respect that co-occurring mental health issues and substance-related disorders are to be seen as the "expectation and not the exception" (Gange et al., 2002). Let us examine some epidemiological findings to support this claim and alert us to the prevalence of this condition. Some of these findings should alarm us to the fact that we rarely see a mental disorder that is not, in some way, correlated to a substance-related disorder. Also, we rarely see a substance-related disorder that is not correlated to a mental disorder.

The highest incidence of co-occurring substance-related disorders and mental illness is among young males, who are single, less educated, and who have a family history of substance-related disorders. Studies have shown that close to 50% of people with schizophrenia had a co-occurring substance-related disorder (either abuse or dependency). Regier discovered in 1992 that 55% of individuals in his study who were in treatment for schizophrenia had a substance-related disorder (Regier et al., 1992). In people with bipolar disorders (bipolar I, bipolar II, cyclothymia), the incidence of a co-occurring substance-related disorder was 61%. In people with a diagnosis of a depressive disorder (major depression or dysthymia), the co-occurring incidence of a substance-related disorder was 50% for women and 85% for men. The substance of choice with this population was alcohol, and this substance was powerfully correlated to poorer treatment outcomes. A note that is to be covered extensively in Chapter 6, the lifetime risk for suicide in the co-occurring population of depressive disorder and alcohol dependency is 60 to 120 times elevated over the general population. This risk is particularly increased when it is accompanied by a serious medical illness, living alone, being unemployed, significant interpersonal loss (aloneness), and interpersonal conflict (Chapman, Specht, & Cellucci, 2005).

Alcohol dependency with co-occurring anxiety disorders complicates withdrawal and is powerfully correlated with vulnerability to relapse. People with co-occurring alcohol dependence and anxiety disorders will quite often manifest additional traits and symptoms of other anxiety issues. Finally, co-occurring alcohol and anxiety issues severely interfere with treatment compliance, recidivism, and relapse (Meichenbaum, 2010).

In a study conducted by the Centers for Disease Control and Prevention in 2007, the incidence of suicide among people with a history of trauma was evaluated. This study used the "psychological autopsy" model, where the subjects were examined after a ruling of death by suicide had been determined by the medical examiner. The number of subjects examined was approximately 1,500, and they were identified by gender, age, race, vocational/occupational status, and religious affiliation. Seventy percent of the subjects had the co-occurring disorders of PTSD and substance-related disorder (primarily cannabis and/or alcohol) at the time of their death by suicide. The issue of co-occurring history of trauma (PTSD) and alcohol and/or cannabis use is *the* most powerful correlate to suicide. It is strongly recommended that when a client who is seeking services presents with a history of trauma and co-occurring substance use that is designed to provide temporary management of the issues related to the trauma that the clinician remain alert to suicide vulnerability. The issue of co-occurring disorders heightens our alarm not only because of the challenge they present in treatment, but also because of the significant risk for suicide.

Donald Meichenbaum speaks extensively about this population. What have we learned from Meichenbaum and others about these people?

- Substance-related disorders and PTSD are the most common of all the co-occurring disorders (Meichenbaum, 2010).
- A majority of patients (80% to 95%) seeking treatment for substance use disorders report having experienced intense trauma (Meichenbaum, 2010).
- Approximately 50% of women and 20% of men in addiction counseling programs report having been victims of childhood sexual abuse. Approximately 60% of women and 80% of men in such treatment programs report being victims of childhood physical abuse and neglect. Childhood sexual abuse doubles the

number of symptoms related to PTSD and addiction disorders (Ashley, Marsden, & Brady, 2003).

- PTSD is three times more common among alcohol- and drug-dependent individuals than it is in the general population. Men with PTSD are five times more likely than men without PTSD to have a substance use disorder (Ford, Gelernter, DeVoe, Zhang, & Weiss, 2009).

- In a study of patients with schizophrenia and bipolar disorders, 90% of them reported at least one traumatic event in their lives, and 43% met the diagnostic criteria for PTSD. However, only 2% had this traumatic event or this diagnostic criteria for PTSD noted in their medical charts (Mueser, Noordsy, Drake, & Fox, 2003).

- Concurrent PTSD and substance-related disorders are more common in women than in men (Hien, Litt, Cohen, Miele, & Campbell, 2009).

- People who have experienced multiple trauma exposures and victimization incidents (e.g., ritual sexual abuse, consistent physical abuse and/or emotional abuse, multiple combat exposures) report greater involvement for engaging in substance use (Bernstein et al., 2003).

- People with co-occurring PTSD and substance-related disorders tend to use, and become dependent on, cocaine, cannabis, alcohol, and prescription drugs (Klott & Jongsma, 2006).

- People with co-occurring substance-related disorders and PTSD show a more severe substance dependence profile and are, universally, self-medicating. They report using drugs to reduce the impact of depression and anxiety symptoms and hyperarousal symptoms (exaggerated startle responses and night traumas) (Ford et al., 2009).

- Symptoms of PTSD that significantly impair functioning and cause serious distress and/or disability are most predictive of relapse (Meichenbaum, 2010).

- People with the co-occurring disorders of PTSD and substance-related disorders are vulnerable to having other severe mental disorders and experiencing legal and medical problems, marital and social conflicts, domestic violence episodes, assault charges, suicide ideation and completion, maltreatment of their children, homelessness, unemployment, social isolation, lack of social support, and report having a life "not worth living." This population also reports having less effective coping strategies and a poorer response to treatment (Najavits, 2006).

- Large-scale trauma events, such as natural disasters, are associated with an increase in substance use (Coffey, Brady, & Bock, 2004).
- Certain subgroups are especially prone to have high rates of PTSD and co-occurring substance use disorders, including combat veterans, prisoners, rescue workers, prostitutes, and victims of domestic violence (Meichenbaum, 2010).
- Certain occupations are vulnerable to vicarious trauma reactions and are, therefore, vulnerable to co-occurring PTSD and substance-related disorders. Included in that group would be medical professionals, law enforcement, military, and mental health professionals (Klott & Jongsma, 2006).
- In a study on completed suicides in 2007, the Centers for Disease Control and Prevention revealed that 93% of the subjects studied had a diagnosed Axis I (DSM-IV-TR) disorder at the time of their death. Of that group, 70% had a depressive disorder and/or anxiety disorder (PTSD predominant). Of that 70% it was discovered that 90% were self-medicating with substances at the time of their death.

Ken Minkoff, who speaks extensively and eloquently on the need for integrated treatment strategies for co-occurring disorders, discusses the essentials of diagnosis-specific approaches for this population:

The quality of any integrated intervention depends upon the accuracy of diagnosis and quality of the intervention for each disorder being treated. In this context, integrated treatment interventions should apply evidence-based best practices for each separate primary disorder being addressed. In addition, a growing data set supports the high prevalence of trauma histories and trauma-related disorders in this population. There is increasing evidence, therefore, of the value of trauma-specific interventions being combined with specific interventions for other psychiatric disorders as well as the substance related disorders. (Minkoff & Cline, 2004)

This strategy is implemented in the context of the empathic, hopeful, caring therapy relationship. When Dr. Minkoff speaks of "integrated treatment," he is proposing to us the need for therapy flexibility. He urges us to look at treatment for this population not in terms of a single style of therapy, but "the capacity, in the primary treatment relationship, to integrate appropriate diagnosis-specific interventions for each disorder into a client-centered coherent whole, with the flexibility to modify each intervention" (Minkoff, 2004). The core task, however, in whatever integrated strategies the clinician develops will be the therapy relationship. I'm sure that most of you have learned the three essentials in therapy: the relationship, the relationship, the relationship.

Based on the aforementioned need for a flexible, person-centered treatment approach, we must conclude that there is no single correct co-occurring disorders treatment intervention, nor a single identified correct treatment program. Each individual therapy plan or program individualizes the person. The only commonality in all therapy approaches will be the enduring quality of the empathic, hope-providing therapy relationship and alliance. For each individual client, at any point in the therapy relationship, the correct intervention must be individualized based on criteria to be discussed in later chapters.

Perhaps the most important consideration in the concept of therapy flexibility is the essential respect for gender differences in co-occurring disorders and, therefore, the need to incorporate this respect in gender-specific treatment. I would like to conclude this introductory chapter by addressing some issues in the arena of gender differences. In later chapters these issues will be incorporated into a need for gender-specific treatment approaches.

Women with substance-related disorders differ significantly from their male counterparts in terms of risk factors, developmental history of trauma experiences, the nature of their presenting problems, the pattern of co-occurring disorders, motivation for treatment, and reasons for relapse. Over their lifetime, women are less likely to seek treatment in an addiction counseling setting. Women with substance-related disorders are more likely than men to seek treatment in non-substance-related disorder settings, especially from mental health service agencies. This has a major implication in discovery and recognition of females with co-occurring disorders (Feeney et al., 2004).

What other gender-specific issues need to be addressed for appropriate integrated treatment for the female population?

- Women with substance-related disorders normally present with concerns about depression (Grella, 2009).
- Women with co-occurring depression and substance use usually seek treatment earlier than men once the substance use is seen as problematic (Grella, 2009).
- Alcohol use in women is more directly correlated to self-medicating symptoms of depression and/or PTSD than it is in men (Greenfield et al., 2009).
- Women with co-occurring disorders of substance-related issues and Axis II personality disorders usually present with a more severe clinical profile than do women with either disorder alone (McMain et al., 2007).
- There is a significant high rate of co-occurring substance-related disorders with women who have eating disorders. Forty percent of women with substance-related disorders report a history of eating disorders. This population also represents a group of women with an elevated risk of suicide. There is continuous investigation of this co-occurring population, with some possible relationships being explored: Substance use acts to service the eating disorder (amphetamines with anorexia and alcohol use with bulimia nervosa—purging type); do they occur concurrently or does one precede the other; or are they concurrent by nature? (Klott & Jongsma, 2006).

- For women, the most common trauma experience derives from a history of repetitive childhood sexual assaults, which was accompanied by multiple accumulative other stressors such as neglect, exposure to domestic violence, and an "emotionally invalidating" social environment (Linehan et al., 2002). In the male population, PTSD appears to stem from combat, crime trauma, and childhood history of physical abuse (nonsexual).
- Exposure to traumatic stressors and the accompanying psychological effects on the hypothalamic-pituitary-adrenal (HPA) axis increases cortisol and other stress-related hormones, which can increase drug cravings. Drug/alcohol use is seen as an act of self-medication lessening the effects of hyperarousal and numbing symptoms (Sinha & Rounsaville, 2002).
- Women who have been traumatized have a more rapid onset of substance dependency than do women who have not been traumatized. They also display more severe demonstrations of PTSD symptoms with initial abstinence from drugs/alcohol and are extremely vulnerable to relapse because of the self-medicating feature of the drugs/alcohol (Greenfield et al., 2009).
- Therefore, there is the need for early screening of childhood trauma, even in those patients who don't demonstrate symptoms of PTSD (Early Trauma Inventory) and (Childhood Trauma Questionnaire; Bernstein et al., 2003).
- Helping women protect themselves from future trauma and/or revictimization (intimate partner violence, sexual assault, prostitution) is a critical feature of treatment for this population (Fallot & Harris, 2002).

We can now begin our discussion regarding integrated treatment strategies for co-occurring substance-related disorders and mental health disorders. Through the following chapters we will incorporate the guiding principles. We will keep the focus on the person and not the diagnosis; we will respect that all behaviors, even those that are seemingly dysfunctional and maladaptive, are purposeful; we will be reminded that people do not change their behaviors unless they are motivated; and we will remember that people with co-occurring substance-related disorders and mental health disorders are the expectation and not the exception. When the discussion of treatment is addressed, we will focus on an integrated style and recall that there is no single correct intervention or program for this population. We will emphasize the importance of respecting that this population has a dangerously elevated vulnerability to suicide and other self-harm activities. Finally, we will respect the need for gender-specific interventions as people experience the challenge of co-occurring disorders in varied manners.

CHAPTER TWO

Definition for Co-Occurring Disorders

All Behaviors Are Purposeful

Many of you are familiar with the categories applied to multiple mental disorders: dual disorders, dual diagnosis, comorbidity and, recently, co-occurring disorders. I think it is time to clean up some language. These categories have, historically, referred to a variety of combinations of mental disorders. We can recall, for example, the comorbidity of a mood disorder and an anxiety disorder, the dual disorders of psychosis and a developmental disability, or the dual diagnosis of an Axis I condition and an Axis II personality disorder, as defined in the DSM-IV-TR (APA, 2000). Currently, in the rather slippery realm of diagnostics, we refer to people with a mental or personality disorder and a substance-related disorder as having *co-occurring disorders*. At this point I would like to expand and clarify that definition.

It has been a terrible misconception that when classifying mental disorders we, actually, classify people. What is being classified are behaviors. These are behaviors that people have, and they do not define the person (APA, 2000, 2013). A comprehensive and vital definition of these mental disorders is given by the DSM task force. They inform us that a *mental disorder* is conceptualized as

> a clinically significant behavioral or psychological syndrome or pattern that occurs in an individual and that is associated with present distress (painful symptom) or disability (impairment in one or more important areas of functioning) or with a significantly increased risk of death, pain, disability, or an important loss of freedom (autonomy or independence). These behaviors must *not* be the result of an expected or culturally sanctioned response to a particular event. (APA, 2000, 2013)

This distress, disability, and risk the DSM talks about are identified by the person and must be managed and controlled, or the person may die from the consequences. Many people chose adaptive coping methods, such as therapy, counseling, and/or medication. Others, sadly, move toward other methods of symptom management. Often these other methods are framed as maladaptive coping strategies. These people frequently discover and rely on drugs and alcohol for this goal of pain management. They discover in drug and alcohol use transient and temporary relief from the symptoms of these multiaxial disorders. They become the self-medicating population. They are the focus of this book and our definition of co-occurring disorders.

An examination of the *Diagnostic and Statistical Manual of Mental Disorders* (DSM), published by the American Psychiatric Association (APA), reveals that most of the symptoms associated with the major mental disorders of mood, anxiety, psychosis, dissociative, sexual and gender identity, eating, sleep, and impulse-control emerge during late childhood and adolescence. It is also commonly accepted that the first behaviors that will mark a person as having personality traits or personality disorders begin to form during late childhood and adolescence. It is also not uncommon for children and adolescents to experience the trauma of psychosocial stressors. For these young people, the experience of any one of these conditions is quite disrupting. In light of these emerging symptoms, they may experience other related stressors. Social, academic, relational, and occupational efforts may become impaired. They may also begin to feel isolated and alone. They may have no capacity to seek comfort or understanding. They also have a devastating lack of coping and management skills. These changes and feelings they experience may render them hopeless. Because of the brief period of time they have been alive, they have not yet acquired what we term *wisdom*.

Wisdom is, basically, knowledge about life and their world. People who have been around for a few decades — and who have been paying attention — may have acquired this essential ingredient to healthy living: wisdom. We know, for instance, that pain and turmoil happen. It is part of life to have things go wrong now and again. We also know, because we have paid attention to life's experiences, that this pain gets better with time. We have also learned, because of our wisdom, that we can cope with the trials and tribulations that life will present. For the most part, children don't have wisdom because, quite simply, they haven't been around long enough. When children begin to feel the burdens of an emerging mental disorder or the accompanying social stressor, they want relief — and they want that relief now.

How do we reach the 13-year-old who can't get out of bed in the morning to get to school because he or she is so "tired"? Who helps the 12-year-old boy or girl who is living a life of terror because he or she lives with a predator of ritualistic sexual abuse? Who comforts the 18-year-old college freshman who has been "disorganized" for most of his life and now, out on his own for the first time, is "hearing voices"? Sometimes we catch these children and sometimes we don't. The opportunities for children to receive the help they need are based on their access to services, supportive environments, and luck, but there is one thing we do know about these young people who are in distress: They will be exposed to alcohol and drugs. Turn on the television to watch a sporting event and count how many minutes it takes before a commercial for alcohol use pops up. During that advertisement, this behavior — alcohol use — is portrayed as enhancing social attractiveness, creating a sense of well-being, and having fun. And then — and I joke here — count the hours it takes for an advertisement for mental health and/or substance use services to be aired. I think you get my message. At-risk children are at greater risk for exposure to drugs/alcohol than to helping services, and with drugs/alcohol they may find the relief—temporary as it may be—for their emerging symptoms.

Self-medicating a mental disorder or a significant social stressor is a process that begins in late childhood and adolescence. The initial goal in drug use may, or may not, be to gain relief from problematic symptoms. There are numerous explanations why people begin to use drugs and alcohol. One basic reason for starting drug and/or alcohol use is to get pleasure, to experience the exhilaration of being under the influence, and to share the excitement with others who are also using (Stimmel, 1991). Over time, however, people begin to experience certain other benefits of drug and/or alcohol use. They feel calmer, more efficient, less confused, more outgoing, less tired, and more creative. They like how the drug makes them feel and, in some cases, the benefits it provides for them. Some people, however, suffer the tragic byproduct of continued drug use: They become addicted. The condition of being addicted has definite physical characteristics. The brain, if you will, becomes quite fond of the drug of choice and starts to crave it. The psychological aspect of dependence, however, also has a major influence on the drug user.

People who find that using drugs and alcohol provides transient, temporary relief from anxiety, tension, sadness, and boredom begin to develop the belief that they must turn to drugs to manage life's stressors. Only in drugs and/or alcohol will these people find release and comfort from the trials of life. How many of you have heard a client report: "When I'm stoned, I don't have a worry in the world"? Many years ago, author Stanton Peele observed: "People with adverse life circumstances are more likely to become addicted than are those with more sources of satisfaction" (Peele, 1989). I am a former smoker, and I often find—even after all of these years of being in remission from my nicotine addiction—that when I'm under stress or in a social setting that reminds me of my days of smoking, that my brain sends interesting messages to me that I would be calmer or have more fun if I had a cigarette.

Regardless of the reason for the initial use of the drug, this person is now under the control of the drug. The person's goals, values, and aspirations become subordinate to the drug use. Everything in the person's life becomes secondary to ingestion of the drug. The person cannot manage his or her life effectively. It is critical, therefore, that in order to effectively treat this population, we capture them as quickly as possible in the process of self-medicating. Readers will recall from Chapter 1 the comment that the median age of onset of psychiatric disorders is 11. The substance-related disorder used to self-medicate usually begins 5 to 10 years after the psychiatric disorder. The key to enhanced treatment outcomes and prevention is early detection. Let me tell you a story. This is a brief recounting of a young man whom I had the privilege of meeting many years ago.

The Story of George

A 43-year-old Caucasian male came to my practice by order of the Drug Court in Kalamazoo, Michigan. He appeared for his interview on time, dressed appropriately for the weather, and expressed an understanding of the purpose of the session. He presented as friendly, made good eye contact, and displayed appropriate thought organization skills and no bizarre or delusional thought content. His affect was flat, mood was dysphoric, and he used an extreme economy of words when responding to the interviewer's comments. Although significant agitation, restlessness, or irritability was not clinically observed during the interview, material presented later by the client's history validated the presence of those behaviors in current functioning.

The client explained that he was there at the order of the Drug Court because of his second driving under the influence (DUI) charge in the last two years. He was placed on five-year probationary status, a restricted license for one year, charged more than $2,000 in fines, and ordered into treatment at an agency of his choice. His probation officer recommended this office for services. The client revealed that he was not happy with having to drive 60 miles one way to our office from his home. He related that his probation officer was "out to get him" and "make my life miserable," but, he concluded, "at least I didn't get any time in jail."

The client revealed that he was married, had a 14-year-old son, was currently unemployed, and because of that, was "close to filing for bankruptcy." When asked how this financial turmoil was affecting him and his family, he stated, "I think we'll be fine if my wife would put some control on her spending habits." He went on to place responsibility for the family's financial problems on his wife. When asked to provide further information about the unemployment issue, he answered that he worked for 20 years as a drug salesperson for a pharmaceutical company located in Kalamazoo, Michigan. He reported, in a rather matter-of-fact fashion, that he had "below expectations" production numbers for eight consecutive months, and so he was fired. When asked to expand on the poor production numbers, he replied that he "feels tired all the time and I have no energy. I've gone to the doctor about this. They've done blood work and can't find anything physically wrong with me." He reported that this lack of energy caused the poor production numbers, which, in turn, led to his dismissal. He indicated little worry, however, about this issue, and he was confident that he would find other employment soon.

When asked to provide a history of his "tired feelings," he responded "I think I have felt this way my whole life." When asked about any previous services for mental health concerns, he glared at the interviewer and replied, "No, I'm not nuts." When asked if this chronic tired condition worried him, he responded with an affirming nod of the head.

The client gave the following history of his alcohol use: He recalled first using alcohol at age 13 with friends. He became animated when recounting that the initial alcohol use made him feel "energized." He reported that as a child he was "a shy kid." He had few friends and spent quite a bit of time "alone." He recounted: "I became the life of the party" after using alcohol. He went on to offer the insight that alcohol has had this energizing effect on him his entire life. He claimed there have been significant benefits to alcohol use for him and, except for the current legal involvement, he did not see himself as an alcoholic, nor did he view his alcohol use as a current problem.

In response to an open query regarding his family of origin, he responded with controlled anger regarding his father: "Now, there was an alcoholic," he stated strongly. He went on to offer details regarding the physical and emotional abusive nature of his childhood, primarily as a result of his father's use of alcohol. He was the oldest of three siblings. Both biological

26

parents were deceased. The father died early in life from complications caused by excessive alcohol use.

He classified his marriage as "a disaster." He offered very few details other than to say that his wife and her family were at the root of many of the family's problematic issues. It did appear that his alcohol use was one of the issues that created periodic family turmoil. He added to that revelation, however, that "just because they think I have a problem doesn't make it a problem. Maybe they should start looking at some of their problems and quit bothering me."

When the conversation moved to discussing his relationship with his son, his affect moved quickly to sadness. To an open offer to discuss this relationship, he stated, "It's not good, but I love him so very much." He added, "I want it to be better, I just don't know what to do." He finished his discussion of this issue with, "I always promised myself that I would raise my children better than I was raised. I feel I've failed."

This client discovered, at a very early age, the benefits to him of alcohol use. His metaphor for being "a shy kid" was, perhaps, his way of defining a childhood depression, a lonely life, and a life devoid of safety because of an abusing father. He discovered that alcohol provided him with social acceptance, relief from feelings of lethargy, an enhanced sense of humor, and a feeling that "life can be fun." From that day, 30 years ago, until the day he walked into my office, those benefits continued to play a forceful role in his use of alcohol. He made a comment to me in a later session that was quite profound and diagnostic: "People like me better when I'm drunk. I'm normally a pretty laidback guy—boring, some people would say. But, give me a few brews, and I'll get you rolling on the floor with laughing." He had a rather constricted view of life. His cognitive perception was that the only way he could function in a social, occupational, and emotional context was with the assistance of alcohol.

When he was 13, and taking his first sip of alcohol, his goal and dream was not to become an addict. Until the day he walked into my office, he was determined to deny that alcohol was a problem and, in so doing, deny that he was an alcoholic. We are going to visit George many times throughout the pages of this book. He represents an example of the self-medicating population. When he stepped into my office, he had a co-occurring disorder. It was, however, his misfortune (because of genetics, if nothing else) that he became addicted to alcohol.

It will be emphasized a few times in this book that people have varied pathways to drug use and dependence. Not all people who use drugs and alcohol to self-medicate become addicted. Also, not all people who use drugs or are addicted to drugs and alcohol are self-medicating. What is essential? The essential is to identify the self-medicating substance user/dependent. How is this done? This essential task is accomplished by a thorough examination with clients of their first experience with the drug and the benefits achieved with its use.

PREDISPOSING FACTORS

People who use drugs and alcohol to self-medicate are predisposed to this behavior. This vulnerability to self-medicate must be captured by the clinician. The identification of these predisposing factors is essential in treatment. The clinician, therefore, must be aware of those predisposing factors that create a vulnerability to co-occurring disorders. These predisposing factors must be treated along with the drug use. If these factors are not treated, then relapse, recidivism, and noncompliance with treatment is to be expected.

Those of us who counsel the drug-using and drug-dependent population make a vital mistake in treating the behavior of drug use while not attending to the reasons for the drug use. People often initially seek counseling for these predisposing factors, and it is only after we get to know them that we discover that drugs are currently being used for management. Studies reveal, for example, that many women who seek counseling initially present with concerns about depression and/or anxiety. It is later discovered in therapy that they regularly use drugs and/or alcohol to manage their discomforting symptoms (Meichenbaum, 2010).

Posttraumatic Stress Disorder

Posttraumatic stress disorder (PTSD) is the most commonly observed co-occurring disorder. Data presented in Chapter 1 validates this position. That data emphasized that trauma victims

28

report greater involvement and higher expected future involvement for engaging in substance use than do nonvictims. This finding is consistent across different types of violence (e.g., sexual abuse, physical abuse, combat exposure, vicarious trauma, exposure to natural disasters) and, in particular, for those who have experienced multiple, consistent victimization incidents. This is, therefore, the primary predisposing factor for people to self-medicate with drugs. Those drugs most often used are cannabis, alcohol, cocaine, and prescription medications. This group of co-occurring disorders shows a more severe substance dependency profile and is extremely vulnerable to multiple relapse experiences.

People with these co-occurring disorders have more severe levels of psychopathology with more intense symptoms for each disorder. As noted also in Chapter 1, they have more life stressors, more medical problems, higher unemployment, and higher arrest records. They demonstrate higher healthcare utilization patterns, less effective coping strategies, and poorer response to treatment than do people with either PTSD or a substance-related disorder alone. They are vulnerable to experience panic attacks, major depressive episodes, and a history of antisocial and violent behaviors. This population finds drug use attractive to reduce the impact of high levels of anxiety and mood disturbances and, especially, hyperarousal symptoms, flashbacks, exaggerated startle responses, and nighttime traumas. They also have a high vulnerability to drug/alcohol dependence. Finally, research indicates different trauma and developmental pathways for this co-occurring disorder by gender. Women are more likely to have experienced ritualistic childhood sexual assault, whereas men are more likely to have experienced childhood physical assault or have been witness to assault as a child.

All intakes for people who present with a trauma history or have concerns associated with the diagnosis of PTSD should be evaluated for substance use disorders. Likewise, all people who present with concerns focused on drug and alcohol use should be evaluated for a history of trauma and symptoms of PTSD. A theme that has been, and will continue to be, repeated often in this book is that if we do not treat the predisposing factor (in this case, PTSD), then relapse, noncompliance, and high recidivism is to be expected.

Psychosis

Research has shown that among people with schizophrenia between 45% to 55% have a co-occurring substance-related disorder (Regier et al., 1992). Data is unclear on the incidence of substance-related disorders with other psychotic disorders (schizophreniform disorder, brief psychotic disorder, delusional disorder). This appears to be related to the chronicity of schizophrenia and the impact this disorder has on social, relational, vocational, and occupational functioning. Although poor judgment and faulty decision making contribute to co-occurring substance-related disorders in this population, their vulnerability is caused by a variety of factors:

1. *Schizophrenia with comorbid depression.* Distinguishing this dynamic from schizoaffective disorder and depressive disorder with psychotic features is often difficult. Therefore, from a diagnostic framework, we advise you to approach all of these categories as at risk for co-occurring drug/alcohol use. These patients often report perceptual disturbances with auditory, visual, or olfactory hallucinations. They often express bizarre content of thought with delusions of grandeur, persecution, and somatic sensations. They also are recognized by disturbed affect (blunted, flattened, inappropriate for circumstances, or a display of the negative symptoms associated with the disorder). They would meet the criteria for a depressive disorder with reports of loss of energy, loss of appetite, or sleep disturbances. They typically have been diagnosed with this disorder for over 10 years. They can demonstrate extreme vulnerability to suicide ideation, intent, attempts, and completion. Their use of drugs/alcohol increases that risk. They will often use alcohol, cannabis, cocaine (crack), and/or nicotine to bring relief from acute psychotic symptoms, to create a temporary sense of well-being, and to escape feelings of social isolation and boredom.

This population has an increased risk of becoming drug/alcohol dependent and, therefore, also continuing drug use to avoid withdrawal.

They present a unique challenge in counseling and are often cared for by community mental health organizations. They bring to these agencies an overwhelming blend of multiple stressors: homelessness, unemployment, no social support, chronic physical diseases. Case management is often seen as an essential for this population. They are vulnerable to multiple relapses and are often noncompliant with prescribed medications. With this population we must decide to be "in it for the long haul." We will talk later about the continuous, hope-providing relationship. This is the key framework for this group.

2. *Age at symptom presentation.* According to data revealed in the DSM-IV-TR and the DSM-5, the symptoms of schizophrenia usually emerge in males in their late teens and early twenties (17 to 24). In females the symptoms of this mental disorder emerge in the late twenties to early thirties (26 to 32). Along with many of other mental disorders, some people have a genetic predisposition to this condition.

3. *Social stigma of schizophrenia.* Studies also reveal that when people with schizophrenia die by suicide, they often take their lives within six months of receiving the diagnosis (Maris, 1998). This vulnerability to suicide is explored in greater detail in Chapter 6. One theory for this disturbing data is the issue of premorbid functioning and the stigma of schizophrenia in our society. People who are genetically predisposed to schizophrenia often have excellent premorbid functioning. They have hopes, dreams, and aspirations. They are often very intelligent. It is not uncommon for them to receive the diagnosis of schizophrenia while they are in college and living on a college campus. The problems appear to begin after the first inpatient episode and they experience a remission of the symptoms. They are aware and come to grips with the impact of the diagnosis. It is here where the terrible stigma of mental illness plays a dangerous role.

Among members of the general population the term *schizophrenia* does not create a positive reaction. Many people associate the word *schizophrenia* with crime, homelessness, and inappropriate behavior. In people recently diagnosed with schizophrenia, this stigma has major implications. They may fear that this diagnosis renders their life dreams and aspirations impossible to achieve. Often the newly diagnosed verbalize fears of the mental illness (e.g., further deterioration, unwanted dependency on family, consistent periods of hospitalization) early in the course of the disorder. They may also experience multiple losses (e.g., family and social support, employment and/ or educational opportunities, financial stability) because of problematic behaviors associated with the diagnosis. They are vulnerable, at this time, to using drugs and alcohol. The goals may be varied: to alleviate loneliness, to relieve psychic pain, or to provide temporary relief from symptoms. Accurate diagnosis of the subtype is essential for treatment and prognosis. The paranoid type appears to have a better prognosis, whereas the disorganized type has the most guarded prognosis. Again, to add emphasis, this special population is also vulnerable to suicide at this time because of the hopelessness they see in the diagnosis.

4. *Schizophrenia, severity index of 3, over time and circumstances.* This type of schizophrenia can be devastating. It is marked by disorganized speech, disorganized thought, and inappropriate affect. This type significantly impairs functioning and may lead to severe disruption in the ability to perform activities of daily living (APA, 2000, 2013). This type has the most guarded prognosis and usually displays a continuous course without periods of remission. It is a challenge for people with this diagnosis to function independently in the community without the aid of case management services. They are vulnerable to drug use, most often to gain a sense of social cohesion, to enhance feelings of well-being, and to provide periodic lessening of symptoms.

Social Phobia (Social Anxiety Disorder)

People who meet the criteria for this diagnosis often demonstrate an unusually high level of anxiety when confronted with exposure to unfamiliar social interactions. They often report that they recognize their intense level of anxiety is unusual and excessive. They normally cope with the dynamics of this diagnosis by avoiding the situations they fear. Their fear often stems from a concern around embarrassment from being evaluated, examined, scrutinized, or judged. They report a vulnerability to panic attacks with or without agoraphobia. They will openly report, often without concern, that alcohol and/or cannabis is heavily used to manage occupational and/or vocational demands for social exposure. They will report the effectiveness of these drugs in curbing their anxiety and how they would not be able to perform without them. They will continue to use the drug regardless of experiencing adverse social, medical, relational, and legal consequences from its use. They often see no need to explore other options to control their anxiety because of the effectiveness of the drugs and the other benefits the drugs provide (e.g., social cohesion, feelings of well-being).

Obsessive-Compulsive Disorder

Obsessive-compulsive disorder (OCD) is an extremely painful mental disorder. It is equally shared among men and women. However, when the onset is during childhood or adolescence, it is more common among males than females. People with this disorder report persistent thoughts and/or impulses that are seen as intrusive, inappropriate, and unrelated to real-life problems. The thoughts are not psychotic. These obsessive thoughts cause significant anxiety and stress and seriously impair important areas of functioning. To manage and control these thoughts, people with OCD engage in repetitive behaviors (e.g., handwashing, counting, repeating words) that are intended to reduce their anxiety, stress, and tension. Also, they acknowledge that the thoughts and compulsive behaviors are excessive, inappropriate, and unreasonable.

People with this condition experience associated problems. They avoid obsession-stimulating situations, and they experience sleep disturbances, appetite issues, and hypochondriacal concerns. They can harbor excessive guilt over their behaviors, and they often assume unrealistic levels of responsibility for events. They are vulnerable to using cannabis and alcohol and excessive amounts of sedative, hypnotic, and anxiolytic drugs to curb their behaviors and to achieve some brief periods of relief. They will continue to use the drugs regardless of negative legal, social, relational, or occupational/vocational consequences. They will reject any suggestions from social support systems that the drug use is becoming problematic. They will claim that the drug use is "the only thing that helps," and they are often extremely resistant in counseling.

Depressive Disorders (Dysthymia and Major Depression)

This is, perhaps, the most commonly experienced and most often reported mental disorder. Lifetime risk for the depressive disorders in community samples varies between 10% to 30% (APA, 2000, 2013). These disorders appear unrelated to race, ethnicity, education, marital status, socioeconomic status, or religious affiliation. These disorders may have an acute episode or a chronic nature.

People with dysthymia will usually report low energy levels, fatigue, low self-esteem, appetite issues, poor concentration, and sleep problems. They define themselves as often feeling "sad" or "down in the dumps." They view themselves as "boring" and "not very interesting." They feel no "spark" or excitement to life. Because of the chronicity of this condition, people actually "get used to it." They will claim that "this is the way I've always been." They are functional. They are engaged in vocational, occupational, relational, and social activities. Because of the chronicity and syntonic nature of this condition, people with dysthymia usually do not appear for counseling. They may report a history of suicide ideation related to periods of "hopelessness."

When they do appear for counseling, it is often because their "management strategy"—alcohol—has become problematic. Alcohol use has resulted in significantly impaired functioning (e.g., loss of employment, family turmoil, legal problems). They continue, however, to use the alcohol despite experiencing these negative consequences. This continued use is largely because they report a significant reduction and temporary relief in depressive symptoms when under the influence of alcohol. This population has a history of multiple relapses after brief periods of sobriety. This vulnerability to relapse results because the underlying "benefit" to the alcohol use—temporary relief from dysthymia—is not addressed in their recovery program (Zuckoff & Daly, 1999). Let me tell you a story about this very common presentation.

The Story of Irene

A 49-year-old woman was referred to me by her husband because of her excessive alcohol use and expressed thoughts of suicide. This behavior began, according to the husband, after the wedding of the couple's oldest daughter. He further claimed that this behavior was "new" and "not at all like her." During our first session together, she gave a dysphoric and lethargic presentation. She reported that this was her first counseling experience. She was oriented in all spheres and did not present any delusional or bizarre thoughts. She avoided eye contact and displayed an extreme economy of words, answering open-ended questions with either a "yes," "no," or "I don't know."

After a while she became a bit more engaged and gave me some interesting metaphors. She stated, for example, "I've never really been happy in my life . . . never been excited about anything. I've always felt a certain disconnect from my life. But when my daughter announced her engagement, I thought that this would be my chance to be excited about something, to be involved in something, to be happy." And then, in tears, she shared, "But it (the wedding) did absolutely nothing for me. If I can't be happy at my daughter's wedding, when will I ever experience happiness? I fear I'll never know happiness."

This woman had a chronic condition of dysthymia that was triggered into hopelessness and suicidal thoughts after her disappointing reaction to her daughter's wedding. Her use of alcohol (wine) gave her temporary relief from her sadness and from the suicidal thoughts. She was psychologically addicted to the alcohol, as she felt it was the only way she could "get to sleep at night." She was resistant to give up this coping strategy and claimed that having a "few glasses of wine actually keeps me from killing myself." People with dysthymia are also vulnerable to engage in pathological levels of gambling (Newman & Thompson, 2003). They will appear in counseling only when the gambling results in persistent legal, financial, vocational, occupational, social, and family turmoil. Despite these issues, they may deny that gambling is a problem. They report numerous, repeated, failed attempts to stop or "cut down" on the gambling. They report feeling "restless" and irritable when attempting to quit or limit the gambling. They often report using alcohol while gambling and will find it helps manage their feelings of guilt, shame, remorse, and fear attributed to the consequences of their gambling addiction. They report a history of suicide ideation when feeling hopeless about their ability to stop the gambling and/or the alcohol use. They predominantly report feelings of excitement, passion, and "being alive" while gambling. A thorough history of this population reveals a history of poor impulse control, risk-taking behaviors, and faulty emotion regulation. They are vulnerable to relapse if the treatment does not address the underlying benefit that the gambling provides— temporary relief from dysthymia.

Another concerning feature regarding dysthymia is that it may be followed by a major depressive episode or disorder. This disorder may be disabling. People with this disorder find it challenging to respond to vocational, occupational, social, and relational demands. They are vulnerable to staying in bed all day. One of the more concerning aspects of major depression is its correlation to high mortality. It is estimated that 15% of people with major depressive disorder die by suicide (Maris, 1992). It is recommended that when you have clients who meet the criteria for this diagnosis, they should be treated as having a condition from which they could die. Of the people who do die by suicide, 60% to 70% either were diagnosed or met the criteria for the diagnosis of major depression. This population often seeks out the services of mental health professionals and primary care physicians. They are very clear and open about their condition, but they will be reluctant to discuss any use of drugs.

Therefore, the questions about drug use must be asked. They are vulnerable to using a variety of drugs: cocaine, crack cocaine, meth, pain medication, cannabis, alcohol. Many people with major depression may not take the risk of acquiring many of these illegal drugs and, therefore, will self-medicate with more readily available, and less risky, drugs such as alcohol and cannabis. The problematic issue here is the vicious cycle. Although these drugs may provide temporary relief from the depression, the long-term use may exacerbate the condition, which creates the need to use more of the drug and the risk of dependence.

Eating Disorders (Bulimia and Anorexia)

The categories of eating disorders are among the more complex of all-diagnoses. Individuals with anorexia, for example, often demonstrate behaviors that are positively correlated to a diagnosis of a depressive disorder (e.g., anhedonia, dysphoria, increase in irritability, sleep disturbance, apathy toward life). Features of OCD are also noted. A significant percentage of people with anorexia express issues of cognitive rigidity, emotional constriction, self-devaluation, perfectionism, and social inhibition. The fear they have about weight gain is intense, excessive, and maladaptive. They also demonstrate a significant lack of insight about their eating-disordered behavior, even after hearing expressions of concern from family and friends (Saxon, 1980). They are vulnerable to the habitual use of amphetamines for maladaptive appetite control and weight management strategies. They can, therefore, develop serious medical complications from methods utilized to suppress appetite (e.g., electrolyte and fluid imbalance, amenorrhea, dental problems, malnutrition). When referred to counseling, they will be resistant to accepting amphetamine use as a problem. They will demonstrate significant maladaptive behaviors while under the influence of amphetamines (e.g., hypervigilance, anxiety, tension, volatile anger, impaired social functioning). They will express terror at the thought of withdrawing from the drug because of the pain of detox, the fear of weight gain, and a significant increase in appetite when abstinent. They are vulnerable to chronic suicide ideation and self-mutilation.

The personality dynamics and associated features of individuals with a diagnosis of bulimia are essentially the same as the conditions with anorexia. The dynamics of the behavior, of course, are different. The correlation to drugs appears to be with the purging subtype of people with bulimia. Laxatives, diuretics, and enemas are often used to purge, but these individuals may also be vulnerable to excessive alcohol use to facilitate the self-induced vomiting. Their use of alcohol is excessive and they are also vulnerable in using caffeine and/or cocaine to suppress appetite or induce purging. When alcohol is the drug of choice, use is often habitual and excessive (e.g., results in severe intoxication).

Dissociative Disorders

I have a few heroes: Abraham Lincoln, Ludwig Wittgenstein, Hopalong Cassidy, and, most important, Harry Stack Sullivan. This well-known psychoanalyst—well, in some circles—passed on in 1949 at the age of 57. His theories live on, however, in various forms and legends. We have, for instance, the Harry Stack Sullivan Society. This group is dedicated to continuing the examination and exploration of the impact of his life and his lessons. Sullivan wrote extensively about the personal impact his mother's depression had on him as a child. He talks about his "psychotic episodes," which led to the belief he had schizophrenia. His clinical focus was with people diagnosed with schizophrenia. He was dedicated to "getting to know the client." His clinical approach was based on interpersonal relationships, and he believed that mental disorders of thought and mood were shaped by our evolving relationships with those in our social environment. He is the author of some insightful and endearing quotes about himself, his profession, and life as he viewed it. Some examples include the following:

"Your emotional life is not written in cement during childhood. You write each chapter as you go along."
"Who is this person and how does he/she come to be here?"
"All of us are much more human than otherwise."
"I do not believe that I have had an interview with anybody in which the person to whom I was talking was not annoyed during the early part of the interview by my asking stupid questions."
"It is easier to act yourself into a new way of feeling than to feel yourself into a new way of acting."
"There is no fun in psychiatry. If you try to get fun out of it, you pay a considerable price for your unjustifiable optimism."
"When the satisfaction and security of another person becomes as significant as your own satisfaction and security, then the state of love exists. Under no other circumstances is a state of love present, regardless of the popular use of the term."

Over the years, as I have lectured throughout the country on the topics of suicide, the treatment of co-occurring disorders, and the DSM, I have quoted this man extensively and, perhaps, too extensively. I have heard that I am often referred to as the "Harry Stack Sullivan guy." I take that as a compliment.

Now, let's get back to our discussion of dissociative disorders. Harry Stack Sullivan teaches us, through his emphasis on interpersonal relationships, that lessons and behaviors learned in childhood are often carried into adulthood. This is especially true, he claims, when it comes to emotional defense systems. Some children experience brutal traumas in their early years. They suffer physical, emotional, and sexual abuse. They are victims of abandonment and neglect. These traumas have to be managed by these vulnerable children. They develop defense mechanisms to keep themselves safe in their tumultuous world. The defenses they develop work well for them, and in some instances, may actually keep them from dying. However, to the outside world, these defenses create behaviors that are viewed as dysfunctional or maladaptive.

As these children grow into adulthood, the defense mechanisms become a pattern of interpersonal relationships. The behaviors, which were beneficial during childhood, have become an integrated feature of their functioning as adults. These patterns are now seen as not only dysfunctional but, in some circumstances, they qualify as mental disorders.

The Story of Clara

This 39-year-old woman appeared in my office at the urging of a local crisis center, where she had spent the previous weekend. She was placed in the crisis center by a social worker at a local emergency room. Clara had gone to the ER on a Friday night to seek services after she had slashed her wrist with a razor. The slash would not stop bleeding, and she appeared to get stitches. The social worker was called to determine risk assessment and need for a protective setting. It was determined that Clara was not suicidal, and a weekend placement in the crisis center with an outpatient referral was appropriate. She was referred to my office, and she was not happy.

We began our initial conversation with her reporting the events that led her to the ER on that Friday night. She said that she and her co-workers decided that before they were going to head home for the weekend, they would go to their favorite bar and have a few drinks. While she was at the bar, a young man approached her regarding the open seat next to her. He asked, very politely, if she had any problem with his sitting in that seat. She told him "to feel free" to sit next to her at the bar, and he did. He did not say a word to her for the rest of the night. But, she reported, she began to feel uneasy because "he was wearing the very same aftershave that the perp who sexually assaulted me when I was a little girl wore during the assaults."

She then went on to explain that as she was being sexually assaulted over a period of three years by this adult in her life, she would "pretend that I was somewhere else." As she was being assaulted, she would fantasize about being somewhere safe, gentle, and loving. Then she added that

"I got so good at this that I began to have out-of-body experiences." As a little girl she began to disassociate. This was her childhood defense mechanism that protected her from dealing with the abject cruelty of this trauma. It became her method of dealing with stress. For her, as a little girl, these "out-of-body experiences" kept her alive, but now she was not a little girl; she was a 39-year-old woman who had brought this defense mechanism into adulthood. The trigger of the aftershave lotion brought back the terror (in a manner of the symptoms of PTSD), and the terror stimulated the need to "leave her body."

She left the bar and went home. She went home to access her cocaine. She had been using cocaine for years to alleviate the psychological discomfort of these "out-of-body experiences." Unfortunately, that night she had no available drugs. Therefore, she went to plan B, and that was self-mutilation. She told me that both activities had the same result—they dissolved the "out-of-body experiences." Unfortunately (or fortunately, depending on the evaluator), she was quite upset that night regarding "going through one of my episodes in front of my friends," and she slashed her wrist too deeply. Sutures were needed, and that led her to the ER and, eventually, to me.

The dissociative disorders, especially depersonalization disorder and dissociative trance disorder, are quite upsetting to the victims and need management. People with this vulnerability often display traits of PTSD, traits of borderline personality disorder, or they may meet the full threshold of criteria for both diagnoses. They have a significantly weakened capacity to manage the stress correlated to these diagnoses. They will use cocaine and self-mutilation (or other maladaptive coping mechanisms) to manage the symptoms of the dissociative disorder and the correlated conditions.

Autism Spectrum Disorder

This disorder presents diagnostic challenges. Although severe and sustained impairment in social interactions is a key diagnostic feature, the same could be said of many of the pervasive developmental disorders. People with autism spectrum disorder also display restricted, repetitive patterns of interests, behaviors, and activities. However, this can also be said of people with OCD, social phobia, and schizotypal personality traits and features. This disorder must also be distinguished from normal social awkwardness and normal age-appropriate hobbies and interests. In people with autism spectrum disorder, these features are severe and all-encompassing and cause distress, disability, and significant impairment in important areas of functioning (APA, 2000, 2013).

The Story of Mark

Many years ago I had the privilege of meeting a young man referred to my practice by a local drug court after he received a DUI charge. He was driving erratically after leaving a local tavern and was stopped by local law enforcement. This incident occurred on his 21st birthday.

I learned a lot about Mark during our few months together, but this knowledge came at a grueling pace. I found myself constantly redirecting him off his favorite topic—the Civil War. The fascinating aspect of this relationship was that I also had a keen interest in this tragic event in our country's history. There were times when I would get trapped by his focus and found myself mesmerized by the incredible depth of his knowledge. Initially, I assumed that his exploration of the Civil War was a diversion and an avoidance of discussing the real reason he was in my office—his irresponsible decision to drive while intoxicated. As he revealed himself to me, however, I gained further insight into this preoccupation. I had to remind myself that we treat people and not behaviors. I had to remind myself of Harry Stack Sullivan's question: "Who is this person and how does he come to be here?"

Mark was a lonely young man. Since childhood he revealed a significant failure in developing peer relationships. He had no capacity to share with me a history of mutuality in relationships. He could not recall any enjoyable experiences or activities with other people. He had, by description, loving parents, but he had no history of forming close emotional relationships with others. His wonderful capacity for insight allowed him to acknowledge that much of his aloneness was a result of his intense preoccupation with that singular focus of interest—the Civil War. He also revealed a history of peer group exclusion and rejection due to his "bizarre," repetitive mannerisms, many of which were on display during our sessions. He would often display irritation when I diverted him from

42

his preoccupation. This aloneness hurt. He was a young man in pain. He displayed behaviors and gave a history consistent with the diagnosis of autism spectrum disorder, which had gone undetected, undiagnosed, and untreated.

I saw this young man much longer than his substance use diagnosis would allow. He did not have a dependency on alcohol. In fact, that night of his 21st birthday was his first experience with alcohol. After a few sessions, he told me that I was his "best friend." He enjoyed our "Civil War talks." He looked forward to our weekly meetings. Our meetings made him feel "less lonely." He continued, however, to go to the bar. He continued to use alcohol. He no longer drove. He would walk home from the tavern.

That night of his 21st birthday was a special event in Mark's life. He walked into the tavern and up to the bar and ordered a beer. The bartender asked to see his driver's license and discovered it was his birthday. The bartender gave him a free beer, and a fellow patron walked up and congratulated him and also bought him a beer. He and the patron began to talk—about the Civil War. For about two hours he and his "friend" talked about the Civil War, while Mark purchased the beer. He began to "feel strange" and decided to leave. He hated to leave, however, because that night he had "the best time of my life." Alcohol and the setting of the tavern provided him with social cohesion and a relief from his penetrating aloneness. It was my privilege to give him the experience of having social cohesion experiences without the use of drugs. We didn't talk much about alcohol use during our time together. He recognized that the attraction to the bar was for social cohesion. He discovered other settings that could provide him with that sense of cohesion—other alternatives to the bar.

Generalized Anxiety Disorder.

Depending on the depth of their worry, people with generalized anxiety disorder are usually very functional. They are actively engaged in vocational, occupational, relational, and social activities. They often report continuous apprehension, worry, and fretting. They are obsessed with crisis; it is all they want to talk about. If they are not in a crisis, they will talk to you about some other person who is in a crisis. The focus of their worry, however, is usually nonspecific and is often not related to any social, relational, or occupational factors. They can be vulnerable to experiences of restlessness, irritability, and sleep disturbances. And, finally, they can't relax. They have no experience with peacefulness, tranquility, or calm. They usually manage this free-floating anxiety in very productive ways. They are always busy. Their activity level is often organized mayhem. Their activity is goal-oriented, perfectionistic, and designed to manage their constant worry. If they remain busy, they won't be anxious. Therefore, they can't relax. If they relax, they start to fret and become anxious. This behavior can be quite disruptive in social, relational, occupational, and vocational realms. This population is extremely vulnerable to cannabis dependency from both the psychological and physiological dynamic. The use of cannabis provides them with their opportunity to achieve peace, tranquility, and calm. The comment, "When I'm stoned I don't have a worry in the world," should be translated as diagnostic. This is one of the more common co-occurring disorders. It is experienced by both the adult and the adolescent population. The prognosis is guarded with this co-occurring disorder because of the acceptance of cannabis in our society and the misperception that cannabis is a benign drug with no potential for addiction and/or damaging consequences.

The problematic issue here, however, is this use and dependency does not come without a price. With chronic use, a sedation process takes place, and the adaptive coping of productive activity is greatly diminished. Users may experience an actual increase in agitation and anxiety, which could provoke more chronic use—and cannabis is an addictive drug.

Bipolar Disorders

This diagnostic classification is awash with confusion. Over the last few years, there has been a tidal wave of clients coming into our practice claiming to have a bipolar disorder. When we ask them which of the three bipolar disorders they have, they react with confusion and bewilderment. We often make contact with the original diagnostician to seek a clarification on the diagnosis, and they respond with confusion. Many respond to our question by telling us the diagnosis is Bipolar Disorder Not Otherwise Specified (NOS). That is fine, but not for two, three, or four years! Our clients deserve to have an accurate diagnosis. And, more important, clinicians need to have the appropriate, accurate diagnosis. For example, studies in suicide have revealed that the highest risk for completed suicide is with the bipolar II diagnosis (Dunner, Gershon, & Godwin, 1976; Rihmer, 1990; Stalone, 1990). We also know that in the realm of co-occurring disorders, each specific bipolar diagnosis may have a drug of choice to manage discomforting, intrusive symptoms. Accurate, comprehensive diagnostics with this population are, therefore, essential.

Bipolar I Disorder

The remarkable, distinguishing feature of this diagnosis is the episode of mania. This mania may be psychotic and is often focused on grandiose, persecutory, expansive, elevated, or irritable moods. People with this disorder display significantly impaired judgment, a decreased need for sleep, disorganized thoughts, psychomotor agitation, and excessive involvement in pleasurable activities with a high potential for negative consequences. I cannot give justice to the destructive nature of this condition in the brief pages devoted to this subject. My hope is that all of you who are reading this book will also read Kay Jamison's *An Unquiet Mind: A Memoir of Moods and Madness* (Jamison, 1995). Dr. Jamison clearly and eloquently delivers her journey with this disorder in a fashion that makes us sensitive to the destructive nature of this condition.

In this state of "excessive involvement in pleasurable activities," people with bipolar I disorder are at extreme risk to engage in high-risk financial dealings, inappropriate sexual encounters, and drug use. They also are vulnerable to noncompliance with any prescribed medication. The drug that has the highest risk factor (e.g., heroin, cocaine) may be the most attractive. Quite often, however, people with bipolar I disorder are drawn to amphetamine, methamphetamine (crystal meth or ice), or dextroamphetamine use because of the stimulant effect. This drug use may result in their experiencing a lengthening of the manic episode and/or an avoidance of the horrible depressive episode that marks the bipolar I disorder. This population is best treated in an inpatient setting because of the potential need for medically supervised detoxification and introduction to the mood-stabilizing medication for the bipolar disorder.

Bipolar II Disorder

As mentioned previously, this is the population most vulnerable to completed suicide. Their use of alcohol and/or drugs heightens that risk. The essential criterion for this disorder, and the issue that distinguishes it from bipolar I, is the hypomanic episode. In contrast to the manic episode of bipolar I disorder, the hypomanic episode is not severe enough to significantly impair social, vocational, relational, or occupational functioning. Also, there are no psychotic features present, as there would be in the mania of the bipolar I. The hypomania is usually marked by an increase in efficiency and creativity. In this population, depression is the vulnerable feature. People with bipolar II will be inclined, during the depressive phase, to use alcohol as a management tool. Because their judgment is not impaired, as with bipolar I, they are not inclined to engage in risky drug use. They are quite functional and do not want to have drug use interfere with the functional aspects of their life. They just want relief from their periodic deep depression. This need for relief is also what drives them to suicide.

Cyclothymic Disorder

This disorder is marked by fluctuating periods of hypomania and depression that does not meet the severity criterion for major depression. These people are commonly labeled as "having mood swings." There is no correlation with this diagnosis and suicide, and when they develop co-occurring disorders it is usually in the realm of alcohol or cannabis. They are functional people and avoid risky behaviors. Their vulnerability to co-occurring drug use will be during the depressive phase when they are feeling "out of sorts," and they discover that alcohol and/or cannabis temporarily elevates their mood.

Attention-Deficit/Hyperactivity Disorder

As was the case with bipolar disorders, it is essential with this diagnosis to distinguish the subtypes. There are three subtypes in this diagnostic category, and each subtype may be an idiosyncratic predisposing factor for co-occurring drug and/or alcohol use.

Attention-Deficit/Hyperactivity Disorder, Predominantly Inattentive Type

People with this subtype of ADHD often demonstrate poor organizational skills and are challenged by tasks that require sustained mental alertness or concentration. They are prone to making careless mistakes in school work, recreational activities, or occupational duties. They have difficulty listening to instructions, following directions, and organizing daily activities. In social, vocational, and occupational settings, they often give the appearance of being careless, impulsive, inattentive, and irresponsible. This subtype is predominant in the adult population and, in that group, there is a risk of engaging in cocaine use to enhance concentration and the ability to complete tasks. This population will also engage in cocaine use to gain acceptance in a social network specific to this drug. This population is seriously vulnerable to becoming addicted to the drug. They will often, for instance, comment on having to use more of the drug to gain the desired effect of enhanced concentration and focus, and they report painful withdrawal symptoms that are only resolved by ingesting more cocaine. It is also reported that college students and some high school students will engage in cocaine use to enable them to do all-nighters studying for exams or completing assignments.

Attention-Deficit/Hyperactivity Disorder, Predominantly Hyperactive-Impulsive Type

This subtype is usually the first observed behavior, and the diagnosis is given early on in children and adolescents. These children are often described as "always on the go" or "driven by motors." Their behaviors, however, are unusual and inappropriate. They are easily distracted by external stimuli, and once the inappropriate behavior begins, it spirals out of control and exceeds the child's ability to manage. They are seen as excessively restless and unable to remain still for an extended period. They are extremely impulsive, which causes social disruption due to talking out of turn, impatience with having to wait, or disrupting others' activities or conversations. In adolescence they report social rejection, academic problems, and occupational turmoil resulting from this impulsivity and restlessness.

They will use cannabis to gain some calm over restlessness and impulsivity and to provide some relief from feelings of shame and anger from social rejection. The cannabis use may remedy the social rejection by providing social cohesion with other cannabis users. For this population, the cannabis use represents significant benefits, and it becomes the primary management tool for life's challenges. They are extremely resistant to engaging in counseling and will normally have to be coerced into therapy settings. That coercion will normally come from the juvenile justice system, because there is a significant correlation between this co-occurring disorder and the diagnosis of conduct disorder. Finally, this group of co-occurring disorders has a serious risk of depression and an elevated risk for completed suicides and suicide attempts and nonsuicide self-mutilation.

Attention-Deficit/Hyperactivity Disorder, Combined Type

This population meets the full threshold of criteria for both subtypes. They will also encompass the full extent of vulnerabilities just mentioned for the co-occurring drug use of cocaine and cannabis. In adolescents the associated features of the combined type include poor self-esteem, rejection by peers, mood lability, demoralization, impaired academic achievement, family and school conflicts, and a high (50%) correlation to oppositional defiant disorder and conduct disorder. However, although they do have to be forced into treatment, studies done by Donald Meichenbaum reveal positive outcomes with this population (Meichenbaum, 2010). The positive outcomes were determined by the client's report on the beneficial, empathic nature of the relationship they had with their counselor.

General Medical Conditions

A basic principle in diagnostics is that all diagnoses begin with eliminating causality from general medical conditions. It has long been held that the first task in "getting to know our client" is to determine if the behaviors we are currently observing or are being reported to us are not, in essence, being caused by a medical condition.

A case in point is the story of a 70-year-old woman who was brought to our practice by her son with the stated concern: "Mom is going crazy." During the initial interview with the client, she was rambling, tangential, disorganized, and delusional. The family claimed that this behavior began to appear about three weeks ago, and they were quite "frightened." They described their mother as a "wonderful" person with no history of behavior correlated to a thought or mood disorder. They denied any history of excessive, habitual drug or alcohol use. When we talked to them about general health issues, they were unclear other than stating that the mother "hasn't seen a doctor in years." Our consulting psychiatrist ordered a complete medical workup, and a severe urinary tract infection was discovered. A few rounds of a powerful antibiotic were initiated, and the "psychotic" behavior cleared in a few weeks.

This is, granted, a basic example. It goes, however, to the admonition of always examining the possibility that concerning behaviors of mood, thought, or anxiety could have a medical base. From a diagnostic perspective, when the general medical condition is seen as directly causal of the thought, mood, or anxiety disorder, then the condition is listed under Axis I. Therefore, my diagnosis for this 70-year-old client moved from the initial thought of Psychotic Disorder CNEC to Psychotic Disorder with Delusions due to the General Medical Condition of Urinary Tract Infection. A variety of general medical conditions may cause psychotic symptoms, including neurological conditions, endocrine conditions, metabolic conditions, autoimmune disorders, and electrolyte imbalances. The same can be said of the mood and anxiety disorders. It is known that mood, psychotic, and anxiety disorders caused by general medical conditions increase the risk for completed suicide (Kelly, 1999). It is also known that there is a high vulnerability to co-occurring drug and alcohol use with mood, anxiety, and psychotic disorders caused by general medical conditions (Meichenbaum, 2010).

There is also concern with the onset of co-occurring drug and alcohol use in people with general medical conditions that do not cause psychotic, mood, or anxiety behaviors. These medical conditions are often chronic and, at times, may cause death. The patients' depression and/or anxiety, while not caused by the medical condition, may be their reaction to the prognosis. Some medical conditions (e.g., HIV/AIDS, multiple sclerosis, renal failure) may have a traumatic impact on patients. This could urge them to use drugs/alcohol to manage the psychological reaction. This population may experience lowered self-esteem, sleep disturbances, loss of appetite, social withdrawal, feelings of hopelessness, excessive worry, muscle tension, poor concentration, and bizarre thoughts. During this time they could experience numerous losses (e.g., financial security, autonomy/independence, loss of occupational definition). They can easily become dependent on sedatives, hypnotics, anxiolytics, alcohol, opioid-related drugs (e.g., morphine, heroin), cannabis, and cocaine. More often, however, their dependency will be on prescribed medications, and they will be vulnerable to using numerous deceptive behaviors to fulfill the need for the medication (e.g., fraudulent prescriptions, theft, street marketing, doctor hopping, sexual favors).

Dyssocial Personality Disorder

Because of the syntonic nature of personality disorders, this population usually enters treatment only upon coercion from the justice system. Therefore, they will enter treatment in the stage of resistance. They will present as highly defensive (e.g., projecting blame onto others, denying responsibility for behaviors, claiming benefits to current behaviors). They also may demonstrate elements of sociopathy (e.g., disregard for societal rules, lack of empathy for the rights of others, lack of emotional response to harm done to others). They will present a history of significant anger management problems (e.g., frequent anger outbursts, assaultive behaviors, lack of internal emotional regulation capacity), and they may report behaviors correlated to the diagnosis of intermittent explosive disorder (e.g., explosive behaviors that are viewed as out of proportion to any precipitating stressors; reports relief from stress, tension, and anxiety after the explosive behavior concludes). They will present a history of episodes of anxiety and/or depression, patterns of impulsivity, faulty problem-solving skills, mismanaging finances, poor employment history, and chronic suicide ideation. The focus of their being coerced into treatment will be either violent behaviors and/or drug use. They have a guarded prognosis.

Cannabis appears to be the predominant drug with this population (Meichenbaum, 2010). They are, however, vulnerable to other drugs of choice. There are times when they may meet the criteria for the diagnosis of Multiple Substance Use Disorder, Severe, with Physiologic Dependence. They will often acknowledge (with idiosyncratic metaphors) that the drug use is motivated, at least in part, by a need to control untreated psychiatric/psychological conditions (e.g., anxiety, depression, rage, rejection, suicidal thoughts). They will present a history of drug use back to childhood or early adolescence, during which they were given a conduct disorder diagnosis. There is a significant correlation in this population with serious patterns of self-mutilation, multiple body piercings, and multiple tattoos.

The Story of Ben

I met this 32-year-old man on a beautiful summer Sunday afternoon in a local hospital emergency room. He was brought into the ER by his girl-friend after he had slashed himself in the stomach and groin area with a broken beer bottle. His medical condition was of concern to the ER staff, and it was decided to admit him to a medical unit for observation. They called me in for an evaluation to determine if this young man was appropriate for that placement. They wanted to know if he was "safe." After the physicians and nursing staff concluded their work, I was invited into the cubical for the interview. The young man was calm, showed no signs of agitation, and a mini-mental status exam was unremarkable.

Lab work done upon admission was positive for marijuana use and alcohol. His girlfriend was present during the interview.

Ben responded to my questions appropriately. He told me that earlier in the day he and his girlfriend were having an argument, and he was getting "angry." He went on to give me a graphic description of his history with this emotion. His bottom line on anger: "When I get angry, people get hurt and things get broken." He then said: "I was getting to that point where I was so angry I was going to hit her (his girlfriend), but I didn't want to hit her because I love her very much, so . . . there was a beer bottle next to me on the table. I took it, broke it, and started cutting. It was either that or smoke another joint, and I had already done that." I asked what effect the slashing had on him, and he responded: "Calmed me right down, just like my weed, only cutting calms me quicker than weed. It is the only way I can calm down when I'm losing it, and I didn't want to hurt my girlfriend." He went on to give me a history of his childhood, and it was not a pretty picture. He told me a story of cutting when he was 10 years old to keep him from killing his cat. "The cat did something that pissed me off, and I wanted to kill it," he said. "But, I didn't want to kill it, so I took my old man's cigarette lighter and burned myself, and that calmed me right down . . . it always has."

This young man eventually came to see me for counseling. We will talk about the relationship I had with him in later chapters.

Avoidant Personality Disorder

It is important to differentiate this personality diagnosis from the anxiety disorder of social phobia and the autism spectrum disorder. Although these disorders share several features and people with social phobia or autism spectrum disorder may meet the threshold criteria for avoidant personality disorder, they have distinct diagnostic differences. People with avoidant personality disorder are driven to avoid social interaction because of significant issues with low self-esteem. They view themselves as socially inept, personally unappealing or inferior, and display excessive feelings of shame or inadequacy. They are extremely sensitive to any sense of rejection or criticism, and they will avoid any social interaction where they fear these reactions could occur. They will only interact in social settings where they are assured of being accepted and liked. They are inclined, therefore, to be involved in drug cultures (e.g., alcohol or cannabis), where they may be disinhibited and gain acceptance as a fellow user. They may feel that this is the only setting where acceptance is assured. They may also find another benefit to cannabis use: They feel a reduction in feelings of shame, tension, embarrassment, and self-devaluation when the drug is being used. For these people the possibility of physiologic addiction is present. The real risk, however, is the emotional, psychological dependence that is based on their view that using the drug of choice and associating with fellow drug users is the only method by which they can gain social cohesion.

Borderline Personality Disorder

This section cannot do justice to the complex nature of this diagnosis. Therapy with people who meet the full threshold of criteria for this diagnosis offers significant challenges. This population is at extreme vulnerability for co-occurring disorders. First, this diagnosis may share features of other personality disorders; therefore, accurate diagnosis is essential. It is strongly recommended that we take our time when applying this diagnosis. We need to get to know the client over an extended period before this diagnosis can be justified. All too often it is discovered that this diagnosis is prematurely given when, in fact, the client has been displaying traits associated with the disorder but does not meet the full threshold of criteria for the category.

People with borderline personality disorder are vulnerable to numerous associated conditions (e.g., depressive and anxiety disorders, bulimia, PTSD, brief psychotic episodes, dissociative disorders). They also have an elevated vulnerability to drug/alcohol use and substance-related disorders. The essential feature of this diagnosis is a pervasive pattern of instability in interpersonal relationships, self-image, and emotional regulation (APA, 2000, 2013). People with borderline personality disorder experience intense abandonment fears and will exercise frantic efforts to avoid any sense of rejection. They often use self-mutilation behaviors and suicide threats to avoid abandonment and to regulate uncontrollable emotions. They also turn to drugs during times of extreme stress (e.g., threat of abandonment) to regulate the emotions coupled with this real or imagined event.

Recall the case of Clara that was discussed earlier in this chapter in the section on dissociative disorders. This young woman was eventually given the diagnosis of borderline personality disorder. She was vulnerable to dissociative episodes and used both cocaine and self-mutilation to self-regulate these experiences.

People with this diagnosis often use cannabis, alcohol, cocaine, and opioids to manage their intolerable stress. Their use of drugs and co-occurring disorder profile significantly elevates their risk for completed suicide. Finally, they are the only people with a personality disorder who will actively seek treatment for the dynamics of the personality disorder. This is a very painful condition that demands relief. People with the other personality disorders are often seen as syntonic in that they cause the person little or no stress or distress. It is quite the opposite with people with borderline personality disorder.

In conclusion I want to alert the reader to respect the issues of adjustment disorders (e.g., with depressed mood, with anxiety, with disturbance of conduct), psychosocial and environmental problems (e.g., support group, educational, occupational, housing, economic), and other conditions that may be a focus of clinical attention (e.g., sexual abuse of a child, neglect of a child). These issues cause pain, and pain must be managed. People experiencing these conditions will be vulnerable to using alcohol and/or drugs for relief and, therefore, fit the classification of co-occurring disorders.

The Story of Anne

This 26-year-old woman was referred to my office by her parole agent. She had just been released from prison after completing two years of a four-year sentence for "chronic prostitution." She was referred for substance use counseling, because it was discovered that her prostitution was drug seeking in its goal. The thought was that if she received appropriate counseling in the area of drug use, that would decrease her need for further prostitution.

She appeared for her first session dressed in very bizarre, uncomplimentary, oversized clothes. She was a small woman, perhaps 5 feet tall, very slight, and about 90 pounds. She was wearing a grey, wool turtleneck sweater that could have adequately fit a professional football player. This sweater came up to her jaw, overhung her hands, and came down to her ankles.

I am reminded of Joseph Sabbath. He wrote about child abuse and told us that "the most terrible aspect of child abuse is that the abused child incorporates the identity given to them by the predator" (Sabbath, 1969). And, we are always reminded that all behaviors are purposeful. The client appeared for her first three sessions in what could best be described as bizarre attire. Then, on the fourth session, I received an opening. It was a very warm day, and the client appeared for her session in the oversized wool turtleneck sweater—sweating profusely. This gave me an opportunity to gently and respectfully pursue an understanding of this choice of clothing on such a warm day. That session opened up a three-year therapy relationship where the client explored with me the most severe history of child sexual abuse I have heard in my 45-year career.

From the age of 8 to 13 she was exposed to ritualistic sexual abuse at the hands of three predators in her life—a stepfather, an uncle (the stepfather's brother), and a half-brother (the stepfather's son). While not going into detail, I must tell the reader that these three predators are now in prison—for life. One of the more detrimental aspects of this tragedy, however, was the message the predators gave to this little girl during the assaults. That message was: The assaults were her fault. They would tell her that she was "so beautiful, so sexy, so hot," leaving her, as Joseph Sabbath tells us, with feelings of guilt, evil, and "being dirty." She believed that her physical presentation was responsible for her pain. Or, as she so accurately portrayed it, my "body beautiful curse." Therefore, at the age of 11 she began to wear uncomplimentary clothing, ignore her personal hygiene, and self-mutilate. These activities were designed to desexualize her body and keep her safe from predators. All behaviors are purposeful. Her drug use was, obviously, designed to provide her with transient relief from the intense, multifaceted pain in her soul.

Predisposing factors are often the reasons for people to seek our assistance. The essential message here is coping strategies. Most people, when faced with a mood disorder, anxiety disorder, or psychosocial stressor, will develop adaptive coping strategies. Many people cannot, however. They turn to maladaptive coping and often exacerbate the problem(s). It is of vital importance that we discover how our clients are coping with their identified hurt and pain. We will find, quite often, that alcohol/drugs are used as coping strategies. They will be the clients with co-occurring disorders.

As we move toward discussing principles of treatment, we must be aware of the cautionary note in treating this population. These coping strategies of drug/alcohol use, self-mutilation, and suicide ideation may appear maladaptive. To our clients, however, they work in diminishing and managing their pain. We are, therefore, cautious in guiding our clients to replace these maladaptive strategies with more adaptive coping skills. The methods we use to accomplish this goal will be the focus of the rest of this book.

CHAPTER THREE

The Core Task of Therapy

Very few readers will argue the fact that the vital component of any successful therapy is the collaborative relationship between the therapist and the client. The therapist may be trained and have an expertise in a variety of treatment modalities, but he or she may be ineffective if the client is not engaged in the process of treatment. The development of this therapy alliance is our "core task." Aaron Beck commented years ago: "All the support and effort the therapist may put forth in an effort to help the patient will make little impact if the therapist has not gained some measure of the patient's trust" (Beck, Wright, Newman, & Liese, 1993).

This comment pertains to all clients who seek our assistance. The client with co-occurring disorders, however, presents significant issues that could make the development of the therapy alliance a challenge. We need to address these issues as we discuss the core task of therapy.

More often than not, clients with co-occurring disorders are mandated into therapy. This mandate may come from an employer, parents, spouse, or, quite often, the justice system. They do not appear in our setting on a voluntary basis. The therapist may make automatic assumptions about "mandated" clients. We may assume, for instance, that their resistance dooms any productive outcome. We may fear a pending "battle" with these clients just to get them to admit to having a substance use problem. And, perhaps, mandated clients and their "resistance strategies" may bring out the worst in us as therapists. We may have to deal with a certain frustration or, perhaps, anger over the fact that these clients refuse to see the harmful results of their substance use.

What do we know about the "mandated" clients who appear before us in a state of resistance? Thanks to the works of James Prochaska, Carlo DiClemente, John Norcross, Harry Stack Sullivan, Donald Meichenbaum, and Ken Minkoff, we know quite a lot. This knowledge enhances our ability to engage these clients in the therapy alliance and actually strengthens our therapy bond.

Recall in Chapter 2 when we discussed the legend of Harry Stack Sullivan. Bring to mind his caution that many of the defense mechanisms we see in our adult clients are, actually, behaviors developed in childhood to protect them from trauma. These defense mechanisms become integrated into the client's personality, and we see them exposed when clients are mandated into therapy. These defense mechanisms, which worked so well for them during childhood, are now viewed as dysfunctional behaviors employed by resistant clients.

The Story of Walter

This 46-year-old client was referred to my practice by his probation officer after he spent six months in a county jail for a charge of domestic violence. The probation officer mandated treatment for Walter because alcohol played a major role in his pattern of domestic violence. Our first session together was interesting and revealing. Walter began by telling me that this legal issue he found himself in was "bogus." He went on to proclaim, in a rather loud tone, that this affair could have been avoided if his wife would "do as she is told." He said, "I work hard for a living, and I have told my wife that I want dinner on the table when I get home. Is that too much to ask?" He continued, "Well, the night in question, she didn't have dinner on the table. So I had to slap her around to get her attention. It is the only way she will listen to me. What would you have done?" He ended by stating, "This was all her fault. All she had to do was have dinner on the table and all of this could have been avoided."

This defensive posture presented by the client may create in us a variety of reactions. Some of us may be bewildered as to how he could actually believe that his argument was rational. Some of us could be angered at his insensitivity and cruelty. Some of us may use this presentation as diagnostic of an antisocial personality disorder with, perhaps, sociopathy. And, for some of us, his reaction may trigger some personal, unresolved issues in our lives that create some significant rage and disgust with this man.

Harry Stack Sullivan would urge us to consider that, perhaps, the client was displaying a defense mechanism he learned in childhood. If we take Sullivan's advice, we may be a bit more inclined to be empathic, accepting, and avoid getting involved in an argument with the client. That, after all, is the temptation—to become embroiled in a debate with the client focused on his issue of resistance.

Actually, I learned quite a bit about this client by merely "accepting" his resistance, avoiding argumentation and debating, and focusing my attention on "getting to know him." "Tell me about yourself" is a statement that many therapists use to begin the process of forming the therapy alliance. This reflects our respect for Sullivan's notion of focus on the client: "Who is this person and how did he/she come to be here?" What did I learn about this man by encouraging him to tell me "his story"? I discovered that he was emotionally and physically abused as a child by a raging, alcohol-dependent father. I learned that he developed, as a little boy, some very helpful defense strategies that, on many occasions, kept him safe. I found that when he denied responsibility for his behaviors, projected blame onto others for misbehaviors, and rationalized all types of misadventures, he was able to avoid brutal punishments. These defense mechanisms worked well for him as a little boy and, because they were so successful, he continued to use them. He was, however, no longer a little boy. He was in his mid-forties, and these behaviors were now seen as maladaptive and dysfunctional.

Donald Meichenbaum informs us that people who are mandated into treatment—and, therefore, are often in resistance—have no better or worse outcomes in therapy than those who attend counseling voluntarily (Meichenbaum, 2010). Prochaska, DiClemente, and Norcross urge us to consider resistance in therapy as a normal, expected stage in the counseling relationship (Prochaska et al., 1983). We are encouraged to welcome resistant clients into a relationship with us. We are urged to recognize them, respect them, and view them in as positive a light as the clients who come to us voluntarily. We are present with them in their resistant stage. We don't debate or argue with them, and we refrain from dismissing them with a preconceived judgement of "poor prognosis."

There are varied forms of resistance we will encounter. We touched on them briefly in Chapter 1, and now we will explore them with a bit more depth.

THE VARIED PRESENTATIONS OF RESISTANCE

No Need to Change

Readers will recall the story of George in Chapter 2 and the aforementioned story of Walter. These two men have quite a lot in common. They both were mandated into counseling; they both were resistant in the early stages of counseling; and they both demonstrated behaviors of projecting blame onto others, denying responsibility for their own behaviors, and they both actually saw benefits to their behaviors. People in this stage of resistance see *no need to change*. They are quite satisfied with the status quo, because the status quo is working for them. This group can be quite a challenge. One of the more significant challenges they present to the therapist is their skill at engaging the therapist in the great debate. They entice the therapist into the debate by disagreeing and arguing with comments made by the therapist, by minimizing any danger the therapist may see in the client's current behavior, and by rejecting any suggestions or ideas presented by the therapist. Have any of you readers been trapped by this population in the great debate over the benefits of, for example, cannabis use? As an example of how this form of resistance plays out,

The Varied Presentations of Resistance

let us look at some highlights from my first session with George from Chapter 2.

Session One With George

Interviewer: Good morning, glad you could make it in. This morning we are going to spend about an hour getting to know each other. Over time I'll be getting specific information, but for now you could start by telling me about yourself.

Client: Well, to tell the truth, I don't think there is anything to be concerned about. It is true that I now have two DUIs and am in some legal difficulty, but I don't see myself as an alcoholic. I was just too dumb to recognize that I shouldn't have been driving after drinking the way I did. Believe me, I am now a firm believer in taxi cabs. I'm just trying to say that just because I have two DUIs doesn't make me an alcoholic. I just used poor judgment.

Interviewer: You make a good point. Your take on this is that a DUI doesn't mean you are addicted to alcohol. Can you give me an understanding of this legal difficulty you mentioned.

Client: Well, as I'm sure you know, I'm on probation for a few years, I had a two-thousand-dollar fine, and I have driving restrictions—like driving to these appointments, driving to work, whenever I get another job, and driving to doctor's appointments, stuff like that. By the way, please don't take offense, but this probation officer sending me here to Grand Rapids when I live 60 miles away in Kalamazoo—that really busts my chops. You can't tell me they don't have any shrinks in Kalamazoo. That PO is out to get me.

Interviewer: I can understand the frustration with the travel. I will make every attempt to schedule your appointments at a convenient time for you. You are currently unemployed? Can you fill me in on that?

Client: I was working for Pharmacia's marketing division. I was a drug representative. My production numbers were below expectations for a couple of months and they let me go.

Interviewer: What's your take on the production numbers issue?

Client: Lack of interest, lack of drive. I get tired very easily. You know, that is a concern of mine—this tiredness I'm always feeling. I've been this way for as long as I can remember.

Interviewer: Have you discussed this with your doctor?

Client: Absolutely. They did all kinds of tests—blood work—everything.

Interviewer: Anything come up?

Client: No, I'm in perfect health. How about that? I've been drinking since I was 13 and I'm in perfect health. I think that's further proof that I'm not an alcoholic.

Interviewer: Well, I'm glad to hear you're in good health. Did the doctor talk about any possible emotional concerns regarding the tiredness?

Client: You mean like depression? No, I'm not nuts.

Interviewer: Yet, I can understand your concern.

Client: Yes, especially since I think it was the cause of my being fired.

Interviewer: Since the job loss, have there been any family concerns?

Client: Finances, of course. But we would still be in good shape if my wife would learn how to operate under a budget. I'm really not worried. I'm confident I'll find something soon.

Interviewer: Any other family concerns?

Client: You mean other than my wife and her family always on my back about my drinking?

Interviewer: I'm sure that can be stressful. They appear concerned about you.

Client: Listen, let me tell you something about my use of alcohol. I'm not a useless bum sleeping under a bridge because his brain is pickled. I have been a very successful professional for years, supported my family very well, and, until now, have been a model citizen. In fact, I think, to be quite honest, that alcohol helps me. It energizes me, makes me more social. I actually think clearer when I've had a few beers.

Interviewer: Right now you see more advantages to drinking than disadvantages. I sense that you see alcohol use as very helpful to you.

Client: That's correct.

Interviewer: Can you help me understand your history of alcohol use.

Client: What do you want to know?

Interviewer: Whatever you would like to share with me or anything you feel would help me understand better.

Client: Well, like I said, I started at 13, with my buddies. You know, stealing some of the old man's beer, sneaking into the garage, that kind of stuff.

Interviewer: How was that first experience?

Client: It was great. Really. I was always kind of a shy kid, and I became the life of the party. But I was careful not to drink too much. I didn't want my mom to think I was drunk. She had enough to worry about with my dad. Now, he was an alcoholic.

Interviewer: Help me understand that.

Client: My father?

Interviewer: Yes, could you give me some information about him?

Client: Well, I'm not at all like him. He was a drunk and was brutal to my mom and his kids.

Interviewer: Brutal?

Client: When he was drunk he would use all of us as punching bags. I'm proud of the fact that I'm a different kind of father than he was.

Interviewer: You should be proud of that. In what way are you different from your father?

Client: I have a son—fourteen. I love him beyond words. We were the best of buddies when he was little. I'd cut off my arms before I would lay a hand on him.

Interviewer: Your son is an important part of your life. Can we talk about your current relationship with your son?

Client: He's sullen and avoids me. We don't talk anymore. We don't do things together like we used to, because I'm so tired all the time. It has nothing to do with my drinking—I don't think. I don't know what's wrong or what to do.

Interviewer: This isn't the way you want it to be, is it?

Client: No, not at all. I can remember as a kid promising myself that if I ever became a dad, I would never be like my father. That my kids would love me and I would love them.

Interviewer: This is very hard on you—your relationship with your son.

Client: Yes, I feel so guilty.

Interviewer: Can we talk more about that feeling?

Client: Guilt? I'm not the father I promised myself I would be. I feel I've failed.

Interviewer: You want to be a good father. Would you like to talk some more about that?

Client: I thought I was here to talk about my DUIs.

Interviewer: This is your counseling session. We talk about what you want to talk about.

Client: Well, I think it would help. I'd like to talk more about my son. These feelings of guilt are killing me. I just can't live like this.

Interviewer: Any thoughts on suicide?

Client: Yes, but I'd never do it. I couldn't do that to my son. The only time I don't think about it is when I've had a few beers.

Interviewer: Sounds like talking about you and your son would be important. Now, I'd like to summarize our session. First, you have been very open with me and I appreciate that. You came here at the order of your PO and, in spite of the inconvenience and distance, you did appear. You're currently unemployed, have some financial challenges, you are dealing with legal issues, and appear to have some family turmoil. You are concerned about this chronic state of tiredness that may be the contributing factor to you losing your job. Alcohol use is currently not seen as a problem. In fact, you currently see some benefits to it. And, finally, I see you worried about your relationship with your son, and we can spend time talking about that. I'm also going to keep up to date on the suicide feelings. I trust that you will tell me if they become overwhelming.

This is a brief, albeit simple, dialogue sample of the process of listening to a client in the resistance stage. His goal was to impress upon me that there is no reason to worry, he is under control, he sees benefits to his use of alcohol, and there is *no need to change*. Most of the interviewer's responses were in the form of open questions, respectful listening, rolling with and reframing resistance and affirmation. The reader will note that, at some points, there might exist the temptation to confront. The interviewer, however, remained empathic and avoided arguments and/or other roadblocks that could harm the atmosphere of client/therapist alliance.

Clients are often surprised and relieved at this reaction; instead of resisting, they tend to be willing to continue the self-evaluation and disclosure process. This form of resistance is quite common with people with co-occurring disorders. They view their drugs as very beneficial and will argue to their final breath about those benefits. In their world their argument is very valid. Their drugs are helpful and beneficial. These drugs assist in control of their mood, anxiety, and psychotic disorders, and they may not be able to function without them. They will debate and argue their points with you repeatedly with the hope that you will engage in the debate. Once the therapist does accept the invitation and joins in the debate, the opportunity for establishing a mutual therapy alliance is greatly diminished.

Fear of Change

I remember a woman I saw several years ago who was referred by a local drug court. Among the many tribulations in her life was the tragic fact that she was living with a domestic batterer. During our therapy she steadfastly refused to discuss her relationship with this man. Her refusal, however, did not come from active resistance. She was more passively resistant in that she was not worried about the assaults she suffered on an almost-weekly basis. She, actually, saw her life as pretty much what she expected, and she knew how to cope with the turmoil of her life. Her resistance came from a *fear of change*. Her expectations for life were limited, and she considered her current existence "her fate." She was not aware of how dysfunctional and pathological her situation was. She was comfortable with where she was and did not want to experience the discomfort of change. She would proclaim to me when I would bring up the subject: "don't rock the boat" or "things are better left alone." The thought of change created a panic reaction in this client. She stressed to me that she had been living in violent settings her entire life, and she was well equipped to maneuver in those treacherous waters. She would often summarize her thoughts by telling me that living with her violent and physically abusive partner was "better the devil I know than the devil I don't know."

People with co-occurring disorders are vulnerable to this form of resistance because of the chronic nature of co-occurring disorders. Remember the data presented by Meichenbaum that points out that self-medicating a mental disorder usually begins during early adolescence (Meichenbaum, 2010). Over time self-medicating becomes an accepted, comfortable manner of coping with stress. In the client's mind there is no need to develop alternate coping strategies. The client's maturity regarding management of life literally stops. Self-medicating symptoms of a mental disorder with drugs is the only coping strategy, and the client fears that no other strategy will be as effective.

Need to be in Control

Another form that resistance takes is anger at being told what to do. These clients *need to be in control*. They are vulnerable to using aggressive, attacking confrontations to gain the control they need in the therapy alliance. They will present as hostile and belligerent while often questioning the therapist's expertise and/or experience. They usually come from a childhood where they learned to use hostility and combativeness to meet their social needs and acquire some sense of control over their environment. They are heavily invested in the status quo, and their hostility is the method used to retain their sense of control. Clients who aggressively confront the therapist with questions such as "What drug have you recovered from?" or "Did you learn everything you know from books?" or statements such as "I know more about drug abuse than you do" or "You're just part of the system that's out to get me" are examples of this group. These people are angry, and this form of resistance is often found in combination with other presentations. They are controlling people, and they often use their drugs to gain a sense of management of life. One important bottom line on this population is that they are deeply invested in making their own decisions and do not like being told what to do. This form of resistance may be the result of childhood trauma or strong senses of inadequacy and insecurity. There are some fascinating aspects to this population, however, that need respect.

First, they normally possess significant amounts of knowledge about their drug of choice and treatment. They are often found with the resistance form of *no need to change*, and their need to debate gives them the additional benefit of controlling the relationship. Also, they may have a profound respect for the maladaptive nature of their life and the need to change. They will not, however, tell you about their worry or allow you to inject any help. If they are going to change, they will do it themselves, at their own pace, and in their own way. They often do achieve abstinence and sobriety. I am sure that many of you are familiar with the data on long-term recovery from alcohol dependence: As many people achieve enduring sobriety on their own as people who achieve it with treatment (Meichenbaum, 2010). I would wager that a significant number of those people who achieve enduring sobriety on their own efforts belong to this group.

The Hopeless Addict

The final form of resistance is very unique and quite concerning. It is usually found in people who have a long history of multiple treatment episodes with eventual failures in maintaining sobriety or abstinence. Because of these multiple failure and relapse experiences, they become *hopeless* drug users and carry significant pessimism that anything you can do will help them maintain abstinence. They are self-devaluating and have given up any possibility of change. They often appear overwhelmed by their issues and state that life in general is out of their control. Comments such as, "So, what are you going to do for me that is any different from the other counselors I've had to see in my life?" or "I've tried all of that and it didn't work" are quite typical of this group. The major concern with this population is their vulnerability to suicide. Because they are hopeless ("nothing can help me") and helpless ("I can't help myself"), they often view suicide as their only way to achieve control of their destructive drug/alcohol issues. They know they have a problem; they have no confidence in being able to do anything about it. Their life view is one of fatalism, tragedy, and aloneness.

The dilemma with this population in their presentation is one of compliance. They avoid bringing any attention to themselves and would prefer to hide unnoticed. They are usually in agreement with all the therapist or group leader has to say and often present as "good clients." Reports of their relapse, quite soon after therapy is concluded, often comes as a surprise. Their compliance, however, is a carefully orchestrated strategy to fly under the radar. They do not want to invest any energy in the therapy process, because their current expectation is that they will fail anyway, no matter what they do.

Resistant clients present in a variety of ways with numerous challenging behaviors. They are quite fond of challenging the accuracy of what the therapist says. They often question and discount the counselor's expertise and authority. They often present with hostile, aggressive behaviors marked by constant interruptions of the counselor's conversation or talking over the counselor. Often they appear inattentive and unresponsive. They passively convey a sense of lack of interest in therapy and are well versed in a variety of other subjects they would rather discuss to sidetrack the current focus. They are quite adept at negating any problems that are brought up in the session and, if problems are discussed, they are usually blamed on other people or rationalized. They minimize any concerns about behaviors and are reluctant to even discuss the possibility of change. They can present as pessimistic about the future and hopelessly resigned to their fate.

ACCEPTANCE OF RESISTANCE

What is our initial task when faced with these challenging behaviors and fascinating people? Our core task is to understand where they come from and begin the formulation of the therapy alliance. The essential lesson from Harry Stack Sullivan is to be empathic to these defense mechanisms. We must integrate an understanding that these behaviors are not displays that were developed by the client solely for you. These are behaviors they have been operationalizing their entire lives to keep them safe, protected, and in control. In other words, don't take these behaviors personally. It is not about you. These behaviors are signs to give an awareness that they are hurting people. These behaviors alert us to early childhood pathology and, for reasons known only to the clients, their presence in your setting creates defensiveness. Harry Stack Sullivan urges us to be empathic, understanding, and, most important, not to get trapped by these behaviors. William Miller and Stephen Rollnick (2002), in their iconic work on motivational interviewing, tell us to "roll with this resistance." How do we present ourselves as accepting and empathic to our clients' resistant behavior?

The first issue is to know who you are and why you chose this profession. Many years ago, during one of my training programs, I delivered the following story to my audience to illustrate the often-experienced challenge of the resistant client. I told them about a client I met who had spent 16 years in prison for criminal sexual conduct—having consensual sexual experiences with a 13-year-old girl when he was a 26-year-old man. He had just been released, placed on parole, and mandated by his parole agent to go to counseling. He was sent to my practice because he would use drugs and alcohol to entice young women into sexual encounters. He was 42 years old when I met him. As I greeted him for our first meeting, he sat in his chair and began the session with the following rant:

"This whole affair was a tragedy. Sixteen years of my life for something that was not my fault. I had no idea that girl was thirteen. She looked like she was in her twenties to me. I don't, or didn't, go around checking the birth certificates or driver's license of women I go to bed with. And, anyways, she was all over me. She wanted it. She seduced me. I did not seduce her. What's a guy to do, anyway? And, you know what, she should have written me thank-you notes while I was in prison. I taught her how to be a woman. There is some guy, or maybe gal, out there benefiting from what I taught her." His language was a bit more coarse, but that was the essence of his message.

When I finished, a woman in the front of the audience raised her hand to get my attention and said: "I don't think I could accept this resistance. I don't think I could see that person for counseling." I applauded her. John Bowlby (1969, 1982, 1988) writes eloquently and extensively on the role of early childhood attachment experiences and the formulation of our personalities and our style of establishing relationships. Mary Dozier and Christine Tyrrell (1998) talk about the role and function of attachment in therapeutic relationships. In that frame, Barry Farber and Jesse Metzger (2009) discuss the role of the therapist as the "secure base" in the therapy relationship. Can we be that secure base for certain clients we come in contact with, or is the risk of transference and countertransference issues too perilous for us to consider that role? This woman, with her own self-awareness, recognized that at this time in her life and at this stage of her professional growth, that it would be unwise to be involved with this client's issues. This is wisdom. A reasonable reframe of Harry Stack Sullivan's query of "Who is this person and how did he/she come to be here?" could be "Who am I and how did I come to be here?" Why did *we* choose this field of occupation. Why was it attractive to *us*. What is *our* story that led *us* to this time and place?

Our patients' varied forms of resistance can be a test of self-awareness. At times our patients' varied forms of resistance can be our most significant challenge. Minkoff (2001) talks about preconceived notions we may have about the self-medicating mentally ill. Weiner and Fox (1982) discuss some of our relationship-impeding attitudes pertinent to working with the drug-abusing population. It has been a practice, especially in the field of addiction counseling, to dismiss the resistant client as "not being ready for therapy." I fear that practice was not designed in the best interest of the client, but, perhaps, to save us from engaging with a person whom we don't like, or who think we are not trained to treat, or who reminds us of someone. If we routinely rejected those clients who come to our office in resistance, we could find ourselves as very lonely therapists.

Recall Aaron Beck's comment that the majority of people with co-occurring disorders are mandated into therapy and, by that fact, are vulnerable to being in resistance (Beck et al., 1993). When we are confronted with a form of resistance that may be a significant challenge for us at this time in our personal and professional development, we are urged, if not mandated, to seek consultation. Through that consultation process, we determine what is in the best interest of the client: transfer to another therapist or stay the course. This decision is not made without serious professional consultation and/or supervision.

The reader may recall in Chapter 2 the story of Anne. She was the woman who had been victimized by sexual abuse at the hands of three predators, her stepfather, half-brother, and uncle. She would routinely arrive for appointments in bizarre, oversized, uncomplimentary clothing. Her efforts in this behavior, as noted in the previous chapter, were to desexualize and keep herself "safe" from predators. And who were predators? They were, understandably, men. She was now seeing a male therapist. The need for consultation during this time was essential. She begged her parole agent to send her to a female counselor. I questioned my consultant as to whether she would be better served by a female therapist. My consultant felt that I could effectively become her secure base. It was a tumultuous relationship for a period of months. She was mandated into therapy and her resistance was profound. She attempted every strategy known to her to drag me out of her life. There were times I dreaded the prospect of seeing her. My consultation saved that relationship. My consultant reminded me that her behavior had nothing to do with me as a person; it was all about what I represented to her. Her behaviors were designed to keep her safe from the threat that I, as a man, represented to her.

As I write this chapter, this woman, who I saw many years ago, is now married to a wonderful man, and she has three boys. She appears, from her Christmas cards, to be living a happy life. I like to think that I played a small role in her development, but then I come to my senses and accept that if it were left up to me I would have run from her like the wind. It was my consultant who saved that woman, and all of the credit goes to her.

THE ENGAGEMENT SESSION

Everyone has a story. We are eager to know about our clients' current state of affairs and what brings them to our office. We will talk in Chapter 5 about the formulation of the case conceptualization. We need, and must have, information, facts, and data. Our clients must have information about the issues of therapy: confidentiality, mandated reporting, boundaries. The inquiry into these areas is often required by third parties and internal review agents. This information, however, must be gathered in the context of a relationship. Our hopes are that this relationship will blossom into a productive agent for change in the client. This relationship begins the moment the client walks in the door for the first session. Our welcoming attitude sets the tone for the developing relationship. With mandated and resistant clients, it also begins with our skillful method of working with their methods of resistance.

Therapy is a relationship of mutuality and reciprocity. Many of the people we see are not familiar with that frame of relationships. We must teach them how it works. One valuable lesson on this topic is to arrange an atmosphere that encourages the client to talk. The more talking the client does, the more productive the relationship is going to be. The more active listening we do, the more productive the relationship is going to be. But we can't listen unless the client talks.

Many people expect therapy to be a learning experience where the client is the passive recipient of our boundless wealth of knowledge. They fully expect that they are going to be told what to do and how to behave. Many clients are delighted when they find out that this preconceived notion is false. One clear-cut method to achieve this goal is to avoid closed-ended, data retrieval questions in favor of open-ended questioning. This method of dialogue gives clients the sense that we are not in a hurry, we have plenty of time, and we actually enjoy getting to know all about them. Monty Roberts claimed in his wonderful book, *The Man Who Listens to Horses* (1997), that "if you act like you only have 15 minutes to hear a person's story, it will take you a lifetime to get the big picture; but, if you act like you have a lifetime to get a person's story you will get everything you need in 15 minutes." This approach encourages clients to talk to us and, hopefully, begin the relationship with the resistance talk. We actually want to hear the resistance talk as soon as possible. We want to work with it, diminish its impact, and display to clients that we are not going to get trapped by the resistance.

For instance, in the case of George, in session one I started the conversation with an open-ended statement: "Tell me about yourself." He jumped immediately into his defensive, resistant stance of *no need to change*. This was exactly what I wished for; to get it on the table, work with it, and diminish its power in the future of our relationship. As I listened to George, I was able to identify him quite quickly as an individual who was satisfied with the status quo, had ready explanations for all of his behaviors, viewed his current behaviors as beneficial regardless of other people's interpretation,

73

and projected blame onto others when issues in his life were difficult. He presented several opportunities to engage in a debate, but I
refrained from the temptation. Instead, I reflected acceptance of his
perceptions and went on a fishing trip to discover if there were any
concerns in his life. He got the picture that I was not going to bite
on his invitation to argue and debate with him. My fishing trip to
discover if he did have any concerns in his life snagged a prize—his
relationship with his son. I would not, however, have received that
gift if I had engaged in a debate with him over some of his more confrontational comments. I would have been trapped in a never-ending
debate cycle, probably resulting in more defensiveness and ending in
a confrontational tone for the relationship. Also, my acceptance of
his resistance was not framed as an approval or agreement of his
position. It was verbalized very carefully to convey a reflection of
his perception: "What I'm hearing is that you see alcohol use as very
helpful." Then we moved on. I did not get captured by the resistance
talk. I moved to our fishing trip to discover if there was anything
in the client's life that *did* cause him concern. If, or when, we discover
the source of a client's concern, we stay there, and this becomes the
focus of our conversation. This is building trust and mutuality in the
relationship.

In the case of *fear of change* clients, modifying their world view is
helpful. Recall the client who proclaimed to me "better the devil I
know than the devil I don't know" as we discussed her relationship
with her abusing partner. Her attitude toward her violent environment was developed by her life experience. She knew nothing more
than violence in her life and, as a product of that experience, had
acquired effective management skills. She also acquired a life view
and expectation that this is what life offers. It is this *life expectation* we
want to poke at and, ultimately, modify.

Various social experiments have told us for decades that our
expectations of life and events significantly modify and control
our behaviors. As recently as 2009, a social experiment conducted by
Dow Chemical and Wayne State University in Michigan validated
this point. At that time a group of veteran Dow scientists—all very

74

learned people—were given a test. Prior to this test they were told that the results would have no bearing on their standing with the company, their employment security, wages, or benefits. The results were totally anonymous and confidential. They were also told that only an anticipated 50% would pass the test with a score of 70% or more. The anticipated and expected average score was 65%. They were told that the test was extremely difficult, almost unfair, and was part of program evaluation. Only 49% scored 70% or higher, and the average score was 67%. The following month, a second group of scientists went through the very same test, but, on this occasion, they were told the test was quite simple, would not take much time, and would not be a challenge to any of the scientists. They were also given the same information on job security, wages, benefits, and anonymity. After the test, it was discovered that 88% had scored 70% or higher, and the average score among the second group was 92%. The only variable of note in this social experiment was the *expectation* message given to the two groups (Washington, 2011).

Changing this group's life expectation may require some time, but it is the essential first step in diminishing the impact of this form of resistance. The reader will recall in Chapter 2 the story of Clara. She was the 39-year-old woman who was referred to me by a local ER after she had slashed her wrist with a razor. She had experienced, as part of her PTSD, a vulnerability to dissociate. She found, at the age of 13, that when she cut herself the impact of the pain of the razor against the skin diminished the psychological discomfort of this early childhood defense mechanism. She also discovered, at the age of 20, that cocaine worked to the same effect. Because of the length of time she was engaged in this behavior—the cutting and the cocaine use—and the many years these behaviors had been effective coping strategies, this client had become syntonic to her current life. Her life expectation was that she would suffer these "out-of-body experiences" until she died, and she would call on cutting and cocaine to manage the impact. End of story. For her, change would require too many sacrifices and become a labor she did not need in her life.

One of the more effective methods to begin the process of change in this population is to move them toward future thinking. This population is stuck in childhood life views and defense mechanisms. We need them to get unstuck and begin to look at the potential of their life. Clara made it quite clear that she had no intent of giving up her slashing or cocaine use. "I've been doing this most of my life and nobody gets hurt," she would claim. She would tell me that no one knows she uses cocaine and no one knows she is a cutter. She would tell me that these behaviors work well to curb the discomfort of her out-of-body experiences, and there is no need to rock the boat.

We don't engage in this reluctance and fear to change behaviors. We do not become captured by the client's hesitance to think of alternative coping strategies and/or comfort with current dysfunctional coping methods. We, instead, engage the client in a mutual discussion of the future as we attempt to change the client's life expectation.

"Where would you like to see yourself five years from now?" I asked Clara toward the end of our third session. I spent the two previous sessions getting to know Clara, and she did a wonderful job in helping me understand who she was and how she happened to be here. She also did a wonderful job in getting into her defensive stance. It is important to remember that we want to see the defensive, resistant behaviors as soon as possible. She impressed upon me that life had dealt her a cruel fate through her abuse history. She also impressed upon me that coming to my office was not her idea. She challenged me on the issue of change with such quips as: "You can't teach an old dog new tricks" and "It is what it is." This question I asked caught her by surprise. I believe she was anticipating my continued interest in her defensive nature. She would sidetrack into safe topics and appeared genuinely upset when I redirected. Finally, she replied: "I'll have to give that question some thought."

She did give it some thought. The next session she came in ready for a reply. She said, "That question you asked me last week caught me by surprise. Nobody ever asked me that before. I've given it some thought, and you know what I would like? I want to grow old with someone. I want a relationship. I want a relationship I can trust. Someone who won't hurt me. Someone who wants to be with me." Then she cried and continued: "And I want to be a mom. I want to have a baby. I would be a good mother." She then pointed to her wrist and continued: "But who would want to be with someone who does this. And how could I be a good mother with this cocaine habit?" She gave me a gift that day, and that gift was her recognition and acceptance that her life was not what she wanted it to be. And when a therapist receives a gift, we never turn it down. We came to this point by not allowing the relationship to be captured by her resistance. In accepting the resistance and moving the relationship toward a mutual discussion of what needed to be changed for her to accomplish that goal, we began therapy. She accepted my offer to learn different coping options for her disassociation.

Angry clients who *need to be in control* present a very significant challenge for a variety of reasons. They are intimidating, confrontational, and can create in us serious fears for our safety. They often thrive on that fear they create, and they may use it to control the relationship. As we observe the aggressive, confrontational tone in resistant clients, our first task is to check on our own reaction to confrontation in relationships. How do we normally work with confrontation and/ or anger in relationships? The answer to that self-examination may determine how well, or poorly, we engage with this form of resistance. Although it is important in this arena to remain calm, steady, and provide boundaries, the most essential issue in working effectively with this group is to give them the controls they seek. Yes, you read that correctly. We give them control that is safe and has well-formulated boundaries.

An example of this population is a man I had the privilege of seeing many years ago, who immediately presented to me his aggressive, confrontational stance. He had recently been released from prison after serving time for a "possession with intent to deliver" charge. He was mandated into counseling by his parole agent. He began our first session by demanding of me a disclosure of any previous drug use.

Or, to put it directly, he said to me: "Tell me, what major drug have you recovered from in your life to make you an expert on drug use?" When I replied that the only drug that had been problematic for me was nicotine, he was not satisfied and demanded to be transferred to another therapist who was "in recovery." He said: "I don't want to see some guy whose only experience with drug use is from reading books and going to school."

Could there possibly be in us an urge at this time to self-validate? Could there be an urge to explain to this person that, according to some studies, nicotine addiction is seen as equally as powerful as cocaine addiction? He then confronted me on my apparent lack of understanding of "where he comes from." "What do you know about my world?" he asked angrily. He continued, "You and your suit and tie and house in the suburbs and two cars. You're light years from my world. I don't want to see you (referring to my race), I want to see someone who at least has an idea of where I come from." Again, there may be present an urge to self-validate by explaining your background of poverty. An urge to tell this client about your childhood in the coal fields of Appalachia, about not seeing your father until you were six years old when he returned from World War II, about not being able to get into a college because your family was too poor.

Instead, the therapist allows and accepts this resistance and gives the client safe control. I responded: "Your concerns are understandable. We do have counselors in our practice who are in recovery. I would be happy to discuss a transfer if that is what you think is best."

The client looked confused. I believe he was anticipating a power struggle. He did not get a power struggle, and now he was confused as to where to go next. So, he continued: "I just don't want to see someone in recovery, I want to see someone in recovery from cocaine."

Now we come to an important juncture in the unfolding resistance of this client. I said to him: "I have no therapists on my staff in recovery from cocaine use. So, what would you like to do?" The vital issue here is to provide for the client only controls that are safe, therapeutic, and obtainable. If that is not possible, then refer back to the client as to how he or she wants to proceed with that information.

He responded: "Well, I don't want to stay here. I want you to refer me to another place." Recall, again, that we allow only those controls that are safe, therapeutic, and obtainable.

My response to his request was: "I'm sorry, but we don't make referrals. I'll be happy to refer you back to your parole agent, and she will find another place for you. What would you like to do?"

Quite often this approach of allowing angry clients to have safe controls diffuses the strength of their confrontation. It allows them to express their strong feelings, have safe control, and, most important, recognize there are boundaries in this relationship and they have the freedom to choose which direction they want to go. The issues of allowing clients to sense permission to be angry, respect their need for control, and honor their privilege to make choices are critical in the formulation of the therapeutic alliance with this population. As it turned out, this man decided to stay with me. What was the initial focus of our therapy? He wanted to discuss issues in his life that were out of his control.

A final word about this group is needed. They are vulnerable to hostility and violence toward others. In Chapter 5 we discuss this issue of potential violence in our formulation of the case conceptualization for people with co-occurring disorders.

We often find that *hopeless addicts* are quite similar in dynamics to *fear of change* clients. They differ, however, in optimism about the future. Whereas *fear of change* clients are managing the chaos of their lives, *hopeless addicts* are in despair and feel a certain helplessness about ever managing the damage that life has delivered to them. *Hopeless addicts* have little, if any, self-efficacy. They are, as mentioned earlier, burdened by multiple relapse experiences that have given them the message of hopelessness. They feel resigned to their fate and powerless about any control they have over their future. They are in desperate need of affirmation and confidence. Miller and Rollnick (2002) claim: "These clients have given up on any possibility of change and seem overwhelmed by their problems."

What is vital regarding this issue is a respect for the fact that people with co-occurring disorders are at extreme vulnerability for relapse events.

Miller and Rollnick (2002) go on to claim that the primary need of this group is a recognition that "relapse is common and not to be viewed as a failure." Prochaska, DiClemente, and Norcross remind us that relapse is a "normal stage of recovery" (Prochaska, DiClemente, & Norcross, 1992). Meichenbaum reminds us of data that indicates that 75% of people with alcohol dependence will relapse in their journey through recovery (Meichenbaum, 2010). Finally, Ken Minkoff calls on us to establish the "continuous, hope-providing relationship" where relapse will never cause termination of therapy and is accepted in the relationship as a teaching event (Minkoff, 2004). Minkoff cautions us to be careful of abstinence-mandated therapy. He prefers we conduct an atmosphere that is abstinence-oriented and not abstinence-mandated. This issue is discussed in a later chapter, because it can be a vital component of the therapy alliance. Much can be learned about our clients' individual journeys to recovery by a thorough examination of the relapse event.

As important as it is to accept relapse in the therapy relationship, it is even more important to focus our attention on affirmation of clients. Multiple research exists that correlates clients' confidence in their ability to change to a strong predictor of a positive outcome. I am reminded of a story told to me years ago by a friend who was also a very successful salesperson. He told me about a new salesperson he had taken under his wing who was quite unsure of himself in the area of sales. He displayed a significant lack of confidence in his ability to market the very attractive product his company produced. My friend, whose self-confidence was his trademark, gave him a list of "can't-miss" potential customers to pursue. He told the novice salesperson that this list of 10 names was chosen because of their readiness to hear his sales pitch and eagerness to buy his product. A few days later, the new salesperson returned to the office overwhelmed with delight and confidence. He reported to my friend the successful sales he made with all of the contacts that were provided. He then asked my friend where he came upon the names of these customers. My friend looked at him kindly and picked up the local phone book and handed it to him. "Pick a few names," he said to the novice. "Everyone out there wants to buy this product if you are confident you can sell it."

Recall the Dow Chemical social experiment noted earlier in this chapter. This salesperson had an expectation that he was going to have a successful experience. This is what we want to accomplish with *hopeless addicts*. Our goal is to instill in them the confidence and self-affirmation where sobriety and abstinence becomes their expectation.

Many years ago, I met a wonderful man who had been burdened by alcohol dependency for more than 40 years. He was in his mid-fifties when I first met him. He had been addicted to alcohol since he was 12 years old, and the story he revealed gave enough information to identify him as a self-medicating alcohol dependent. He was referred to treatment by his parole agent, because his alcohol use had resulted in him being involved in the justice system. He had a very long treatment history, followed by recurrent relapse events.

After I welcomed him into my office to begin our first session together, he sat down and said: "So, what are you going to do for me that's going to be different from the 10 other counselors I've seen in my miserable life?" One of the comments that Harry Stack Sullivan is known for and that certainly comes into play with the *hopeless addict* is "no one is as incompetent as they appear" (Sullivan, 1954). In other words, everyone has strengths. It is just a matter of finding them. Sometimes we find those strengths in the strangest places.

I replied: "Really, 10 other counselors? That is fascinating. Could you tell me about the most recent treatment experience? What was it like? What happened?" Our clients' strengths are found in their history. Everyone has a story. As we listen to our clients' stories, they may reveal an essential strength that may alter their self-perception and begin the process of changing their life expectations.

The client tells me: "Sure, I'll tell you what happened. It was last year. My PO tells me, once again, to get counseling because I had another of my famous relapses. So, he sends me to this guy down in Middleville. Now, I have to tell you something. You people make me nervous. I really don't like you people poking around in my life. My life is my business, not yours. What I do is, really, none of your business. Anyway, like I said, you people make me nervous. And when I get nervous, I need a beer. Beer calms me down. So before I went to see this guy, I stopped at the bar and had a few. Had to calm my nerves so I could talk to this man."

"What happened?" I asked.

"I'll tell you what happened," he continued. "I get to the guy's office and the first thing he asks me is 'Have you been abstinent?' I'm thinking he's asking me about my sex life, you know, so I told him that I haven't been abstinent and that my girlfriend and I did it just last night! The guy turns red and says he was asking if I was remaining sober. How was I supposed to know what he meant with that word? So, anyway, I said to him that I had a few beers before I came to his office and I told him the reason, like I just told you, because of my nerves."

"What happened?" I asked.

"I'll tell you what happened," he continued. "The guy calls my PO and reports my drinking. My PO is tired of me and can't wait until I get off paper (off parole). So he sends me to TRV (Technical Rules Violation Center for violators of stipulations of parole) for three months. I lost my job, lost my house, and my girlfriend quits on me."

He then glares at me and says: "So, buddy, as I said to you—what are you going to do any different than the other counselors I have had the privilege of meeting over the years? You know, I have been in counseling since I was twelve years old. How about that?"

I spoke: "Well, thank you for that story. I have to tell you I am impressed."

"Impressed?" he replied. "What are you impressed with?"

"Your honesty," I said. "When that counselor asked about your sobriety, you honestly told him you had been drinking and you told him why. You did the same for me, thank you. You appear to be an honest man."

"Nobody has ever said that to me before," he said.

That very brief interaction began a process in our relationship of self-efficacy for the client and the evolution of a change in his life expectation. He began, slowly, to trust himself to work once again on a sober lifestyle.

Before we leave our conversation on mandated and resistant clients, it is important to address what I consider to be a myth among clinicians concerning highly at-risk clients. I have often heard that when people are at serious risk (crack-dependent psychotic or the pregnant cocaine user) that more intense interventions must be used when they present as resistant. Those who advocate this approach will claim that time is not on our side, and we must act quickly, decisively, and forcefully to save these people from themselves. It is also argued by some clinicians that we "don't have the time" to exercise these interesting skills. It is advocated that more intense treatment, more coercion, more confrontation is called for. In some cases, that may be a good point. Certainly, the psychotic cocaine user, who desires to spend the night outdoors when the temperature is below zero, needs mandated care.

But these decisions need to be made cautiously. Actually, studies done by Miller and Rollnick and others validate that "more is not better." These studies reveal that when coercion is forcefully applied to people in resistance that the efforts of coercion actually create *more* resistance and draw the person farther away from the clinician and the goals of treatment (Heather, Rollnick, & Bell, 1996; Miller, Benefield, & Tonigan, 1998). These studies advocate that we avoid common misguided practices originally designed to force resistant clients into treatment compliance. The strategies that were noted were tactics of arguing, shaming, blaming, criticizing, emotional blackmail, and demeaning the client. It is argued that in emergency conditions these strategies are essential because time is limited. The problem with that argument is that not one shred of evidence validates that claim.

At all times we are reminded that these relationships we have established are the clients' therapy. They do with this relationship whatever they feel they need to at this time in their lives. Clients should never "have to" do anything in their relationship with us. They should, above all, remain autonomous. They must believe, based on the spirit of our relationship, that abstinence/sobriety is their choice and their decision, and we respect whatever decision they make.

CHAPTER FOUR

The Therapy Alliance
Nobody Changes Without Motivation

In previous chapters we have noted the challenge of treatment for the self-medicating mentally ill. We have documented the data on the prevalence of drug and alcohol use among people with diagnosed mental disorders. Studies consistently reveal that people with co-occurring disorders are, historically, less adherent with psychological and pharmacological interventions than others who are engaged in mental health care (Jerrell & Ridgely, 1995). Several factors play a role in this rather depressing data. Substance use among people with a mental illness often compromises the efficacy of prescribed medications and often exacerbates the symptoms of the mental disorder. This dynamic can, therefore, cause a need for numerous periods of inpatient care, along with noncompliance with treatment. Substance use can further impair clients' judgment and reasoning, while increasing their risk-taking behaviors and, therefore, putting them in harm's way.

Another factor that contributes to the challenge of effective treatment for this population is the historic lack of coordination in programs. Often this population was caught in the vicious game of human volleyball. They would seek treatment, for example, for the symptoms of a mental disorder and be told, once it was discovered they had a co-occurring substance use issue, that they could not be receive mental health treatment until their substance use issue was under control. So, off they would go to a substance use disorder program only to be told, once it was discovered they had a co-occurring mental health concern, that they could not be treated by the substance disorder program until their mental health concerns were under control. I would imagine that this sounds quite familiar to many readers. Clients who were caught in this game became frustrated, angry, and hopeless. There is no question that lack of coordination between the two (substance use treatment and mental health treatment) service systems has led to poor treatment engagement, high drop-out rates, and relapse among the dually diagnosed (Handmaker, Packard, Conforti, 2002).

To the rescue come new programs that integrated substance use treatment with mental health treatment. With this focus, alcohol and drug treatment programs are incorporated into existing psychiatric, nursing, counseling, and case-management services provided by multidisciplinary teams in either hospital or community-based settings. Some of our brightest clinicians contributed to the dynamics and research of these well-planned, well-thought-out programs. The results, however, were disappointing. Some reviews revealed, for instance, that integrated care showed only a slight outcome improvement over the prior nonintegrated approaches (Drake, Mercer, Mueser, McHugo, & Bond, 1999). An example from one study showed drop-out rates of more than 80% in residential programs offering integrated treatment for the self-medicating mentally ill (Drake et al., 1999). Why are we having these results? It is largely because no one changes behaviors without motivation.

We have available to us marvelous treatment programs from the likes of Ken Minkoff, Donald Meichenbaum, and Case Western Reserve University that were designed to greatly improve the lives of people with co-occurring disorders. All of these programs have a component devoted to motivation. Without motivation, there is no change in behaviors. The key question, with people who self-medicate, is how do we accomplish this task of motivating our clients to engage in and remain compliant with treatment programs that offer an excellent chance of success. This discussion is essential. People with co-occurring disorders often are mandated into programs; therefore, they often engage in treatment with hesitancy and resistance. We previously spoke of issues in working with mandated and resistant clients. Let us now focus our attention on motivation.

In my career I have gained a valuable lesson on the issue of motivation. In the early stages of my career — more than 45 years ago — I believed I was motivating clients when I criticized them, found fault with their judgment, and, in general, treated them with a tragic lack of respect. I commented on this process in Chapter 1. I believed that this approach would motivate them to change behaviors. Instead, it made their resistance stronger. Then I approached them through education. I pointed out to my clients the danger they placed themselves in by using drugs and alcohol. I showed them films of their "brains on drugs." I had them read the tragic data on chronic drug use and how it robs us of health, family, and self-respect.

Finally, through the gift given to me by William Miller and Stephen Rollnick, I realized my mistake. Therapists do not motivate clients. Motivation for change is not instilled into clients by the counselor. People motivate themselves. The counselor merely arranges an appropriate atmosphere where the clients begin to recognize that their current behaviors are severely damaging their opportunity to have a life worth living. For change to be enduring and to diminish the threat of relapse, clients must discover the motivation to change their behaviors. Motivation that is instilled onto us by others will be short lived, lack endurance, and fade very quickly. Furthermore, this discovery clients make to motivate them to change must be based on something they value, treasure, or want in their lives.

Many of you may recall the wonderful book by Kenneth Grahame, *The Wind in the Willows*. Grahame wrote this book in 1908 for his partially blind son, Alastair. If we read it closely, however, it holds numerous lessons for people and their lives. One of the characters, Toad, was a rich, jolly fellow who thoroughly enjoyed life and, especially, motorcars. The problem was that he was quite impulsive and careless—not good qualities for a person who enjoyed racing at very high speeds. Therefore, one day, two of his better friends, Badger and Rat, decided it was time for an intervention to get Toad off the roads before he hurt someone. Grahame's telling of this intervention was classic, and it almost parallels what we do today to motivate people with addictions to change behaviors. The story also tells of the very same outcome we could expect today when we attempt to instill motivation upon a person to change behaviors.

The goal of this intervention was to teach Mr. Toad to be a "sensible Toad." Badger said, "I am going to change and straighten out his miserable life today!" Badger then proceeded to take Toad "firmly by the arm, led him into the library, and closed the door behind them." After 45 minutes the door opened, with Badger triumphantly proclaiming: "Toad has seen the folly of his ways; haven't you Toad?" Then there was a very long, long pause. "No!" Toad said. Badger was in disbelief. "But, you promised in there to change," cried Badger. Toad responded: "I'd have said anything in there." Trying to motivate people to change by using coercion, interventions, or installation tactics are not successful. These strategies are proven to be failures even in fantasy literature.

Let me tell you a brief story from my life to make my point. I am nicotine dependent. I have been in remission for many years, but I still experience a craving now and then. My change from using to remission came slowly and in varied increments. I recall my very first attempt at curbing my nicotine habit occurred when my children were very young. One winter in my neck of the woods, we were attacked by a vicious snowstorm that brought us a three-day blizzard with more than three feet of snow. Nothing was moving. My wife, who was employed at a local hospital, was trapped and could not leave her medical unit. I was stranded, at home, with three children ages 5, 3, and 1. And I ran out of cigarettes. Did I mention that nothing was moving? I called various stores to see if anything was open, and my fervent prayers were answered. One store, a mom-and-pop convenience store not too far from where I lived was open because the owners lived on the second floor of the store. They said they would be happy to sell me some smokes if I could get to the store. At that time there was no question that I was going to get to the store. So began the famous family tradition of telling the story of the sled ride. Our five children are now in their thirties and forties and have given us eight wonderful grandchildren. This story remains alive with both laughter and disbelief.

"Let's go, guys! We're going for a sled ride," I said to these three wide-eyed little ones who, initially, were thrilled about the prospect of going out into the snow. The temperature was in the teens, the wind was howling, and the snow was drifting. But, my street was plowed, and all I had to do was to make it out to the street! So, I bundled these three wonderful children as warm as possible and opened the door. I was going to get my drug. The biting cold and the bitter wind was nothing compared to the wave of self-loathing that hit me as I tried to take them outside. I made it about 10 feet out the door and came back. The thought hit me — and I will never forget it until my dying day — that "fathers do not do this to their children." This act I was about to perform contradicted my deeply engrained value of "being a good father." William Miller and Stephen Rollnick would have told me that, at that moment, I discovered my discrepancy. I discovered on that bitterly cold, snowy morning that my behavior violated something I cherished and valued in my life — my role as a parent. I quit smoking for three years after that day.

Be aware that I did *not* quit smoking for my children. People don't change behaviors for other people. Many people would claim that I quit for the kids. I imagine that some of you reading this chapter have heard people ask addicted friends, "Won't you do it for your family?"

I quit smoking in order to have a sense of genuine integrity in my role as a father. I quit so I could feel better about myself. Stopping inappropriate behaviors for other people runs a risk of being very fragile motivation. It is also motivation that is externalized from the person. For behavioral change to be enduring and secure, the motivation to change must be internalized, intimate, and from the heart — it is person-centered motivation.

In previous chapters we commented on the guidance given us by Edwin Shneidman. He urges us to always focus on the locus of clients' pain. He tells us that our first task is to discover where clients hurt and assist in helping them acquire management skills. The pain he speaks of will often be the discrepancy in people's lives; their life is not the way they wanted it to be. This discrepancy often becomes the essence of the motivation our clients need to change behaviors. Discover the locus of the clients' pain and, quite often, we have discovered the route to the motivation to change behaviors.

This pain is discovered by strategies that were mentioned in previous chapters:

1. Never get involved in the client's resistance behaviors
2. Always remain empathic to the client
3. Remember that therapy is a mutual relationship
4. Always be a listener and not a talker
5. Look for opportunities to affirm your client
6. Use the Socratic Method of interview by asking open-ended questions that encourage the client to converse

We are now going to examine the case of George a bit more closely. This man came to my office at the mandate of his probation officer. He appeared, therefore, for his first session in a stage of resistance. As we spoke about him in Chapters 2 and 3, we discussed the form of resistance that he displayed. He was a rationalizer. He projected blame onto others, rationalized his own behaviors, found benefits to his current behaviors, and completely refused to see his current behaviors as problematic. He had no motivation to change. We will now revisit him to explore how he discovered his discrepancy in further sessions and became motivated to change his behaviors.

THE STORY OF GEORGE

In the first session we recorded in Chapter 3 a sample of eliciting the discrepancy as a means for building motivation for change. Most of the interviewer's responses were in the form of open questions, respectful listening, and rolling with and reframing resistance and affirmation. The reader will note that, at some points, the interviewer might be tempted to confront. The interviewer, however, remained empathic and avoided arguments and/or other roadblocks that could harm the atmosphere of client-generated problem identification. Clients are often surprised and relieved at this approach; instead of resisting, they tend to be willing to continue the self-evaluation/disclosure process.

The client has identified "where he hurts," and the interviewer invites him to go there. This hurt is coupled with a major discrepancy in the client's life — to be a good father. This is enough motivation to where the client is invited to explore the hurt (guilt). Now the interviewer implements aspects of treatment to assist the client in emotional regulation and distress tolerance of the guilt. The interviewer is *not* ignoring the alcohol use (abuse/dependency) nor the depressive disorder nor the obvious interaction between the two. They are both in resistance and will be treated accordingly when the client is in a stage of readiness to work on those issues.

Session Two With George

Interviewer: I'm glad to see you. How has your week been?

Client: Miserable. My wife just won't leave it alone about the drinking and the DUIs, I think her sister is encouraging her to divorce me, and my son is at the point where he walks out of the room when I walk in.

Interviewer: It sounds very stressful—and very frightening.

Client: That's a good word—frightening. I can't take all of this: DUIs, no job, money problems, wife problems, kid problems.

Interviewer: How are you managing all of this?

Client: I hide, seriously. I stay in bed most of the day. I don't sleep, I just stay in bed. And then at night I go to the bar and hang out with my buddies. I'll tell you, thank heavens for them. Going to the bar at night is the only thing keeping me sane.

Interviewer: How is that working for you, and how are the suicidal thoughts?

Client: You mean staying in bed and going to the bar?

Interviewer: Yes, as coping strategies, how are they working for you?

Client: Well, for one thing, my buddies make me feel better—feel better about myself. And the alcohol, well, the alcohol makes the pain numb.

Interviewer: The pain—the guilt—we touched on previously? The alcohol numbs the guilt?

Client: Okay, you could say that.

Interviewer: Based on what we talked about, that is what I'm hearing. Can we talk more about you and this feeling of guilt?

Client: Well, I'm good at it, feeling guilt and shame. I learned from the master, my old man. He never let go of a chance to find something wrong with me.

Interviewer: I can understand you feeling all types of emotions when we look at your early experiences—anger, shame, guilt— they are all very understandable. And also what is understandable is your need to manage these emotions, and you found alcohol very useful.

Client: Okay, since you put it that way. I see where you're going.

Interviewer: It's a confusing situation, isn't it? That which has helped you manage pain for most of your life can also create havoc in your life, like the DUI.

Client: I don't know. You take the good with the bad, I guess.

Interviewer: Are you open to talking about other ways to manage this guilt?

Client: And quit drinking? There is more to my drinking than just making me feel better. I like the taste, and I bond through Budweiser.

Interviewer: Giving you options, so that if, or when, you decide that alcohol is not in your best interest, you have other ways to manage the pain that life brings and, maybe, different ways to form relationships.

Client: So, you're not telling me I have to quit drinking tomorrow. I think you're trying to tell me that I drink for a number of reasons.

Interviewer: Correct.

Client: I've felt like this my whole life . . . that I fail at everything . . . I'm worthless. How can I get rid of that?

Interviewer: Not "get rid of"—that's what alcohol does, for a short time. We're talking management, not elimination, and we'll talk about it, and we'll keep talking until we find what works to help you.

Client: I hope it works.

Interviewer: Well, what we've done today is focus on this guilt/shame issue, which could be one of the factors that makes alcohol so helpful and attractive to you. We've agreed to look at other ways to manage these very common, understandable, and painful feelings, and we are going to talk about some things and see if they work for you. And, if they don't, we'll keep talking until we find what works.

The therapy moved because of a major motivating discrepancy being discovered rather quickly, and the interviewer decided to act on it. Remember, going to where the client hurts is the first order of business. The interviewer, using some select skills, moved and generated the client's desire to move toward skills enhancement in emotional regulation, distress tolerance, and relationship effectiveness.

Session Three With George

Interviewer: Good to see you. How was this past week?

Client: Well, both good and bad.

Interviewer: A lot like life.

Client: I guess. I've tried some of the skills we talked about, but the tavern called out my name last night.

Interviewer: Well, let's talk about it.

Client: My wife and I had a huge fight over one of her credit card bills. And then my son called me the same name I used to call my old man when he was drunk. That was way too much. I tried the opposite-to-emotion thing we talked about. I tried to repair the situation by apologizing to my wife for my anger, and I did feel better, but then she attacked me for being a phony, and I just left the house and went to the bar.

Interviewer: That must have been disappointing. What did you learn?

Client: Well, I'm paying much more attention to myself. I trigger into rage when I'm not in control of things, and when my wife spent that money without checking with me first, I went nuts. And then my son's name-calling . . .

Interviewer: Sounds like you handled it well. What did you enter in your journal last night?

Client: Well, alcohol is my best friend. It has great advantages for me. It helps me gain friends, helps me feel better about myself, helps me forget painful stuff, and I like the taste. But, I think, I'm paying a price for this — my son. I love that kid beyond words. Do you want to hear a story? You know when I promised myself that

I would be a better father than my old man? He had just beaten me senseless. I was thirteen . . . he broke my jaw, wrist, and two ribs. Before I got to the hospital, lying on my bed, I made that promise.

Interviewer: This isn't the way you wanted to be, is it? I have a sense that you are at your best, and happiest, when you and your son are doing well together. I think, in a way, raising your son is your passion.

Client: I think that's true. My happiest moments are when I am with him, when I see him happy. I fear I've lost him, that's the shame. I've screwed up the most fun and important job I'll ever have.

Interviewer: I think it might be helpful to look at some things that might help repair this relationship. We are certainly going to continue looking at your shame and how it controls some of your behaviors, but I sense you want to talk also about this relationship. Let's do that.

The door is open, with the therapist using aspects of treatment to help repair this relationship. Work now will focus on behavioral strategies by which the client may operate in a constructive fashion with his son. Continued insight may be provided by the client on the influence of shame on his actions and how to manage this emotion with reminders of his skill sets. And, we *are not* ignoring the issues of alcohol and depression in the client's life. These issues remain in resistance. It is the client's responsibility, not the therapist's, to discover the role that alcohol plays both in his depression and his relationship with his son. He must discover the motivation to change for his change to be enduring.

Session Four With George

Interviewer: Nice to see you. How has your week been?

Client: My son walks out of the room when I walk in. What does that tell you about how my week has been?

Interviewer: You have feelings of anger, and based on what we have been talking about, what other feelings are experienced when he does that?

Client: Those feelings of shame and guilt come up, and then all I want to do is get to the bar and be with my buddies and down a few beers to calm down. I know all that. But—and I hope you believe this—I have not been going to the bar that often. I've been using that self-soothing stuff we've been talking about, and it seems to help.

Interviewer: You are using some other ways to manage your guilt other than alcohol. Remember, feelings just are, they don't define us. The alcohol is used to eliminate, briefly, those uncomfortable emotions. The skills you are practicing will help in managing those emotions.

Client: I guess, but what do I do about him? I'm taking care of me, but what about my relationship with him? You know, not long ago we used to have a routine of having breakfast together. But while he was eating cereal, I was having my jumpstart breakfast—two fingers of Jim Beam and two Buds, that was my breakfast. I quit doing that because he was complaining to his mother about it, and because I would do anything to make him happy.

Interviewer: How long ago did that happen? When you quit your jumpstart breakfast?

Client: About nine months before I was fired.

Interviewer: I see, and now what has been happening?

Client: He doesn't eat with me at all . . . he totally avoids me . . . just like I avoided my old man. He pretends I don't exist. I just want him back. I want him to be my buddy again.

Interviewer: This avoiding you . . . that appears to be the major problem in the relationship. You just want a chance to do things with him again.

Client: That's it, right there.

Interviewer: Let's talk about a few things to make that happen. What changes would you like to see?

Client: I don't know. We used to do all kind of things together. We were joined at the hip, I want to go back to that.

Interviewer: What can we discuss to make that happen?

Client: Well, we both love baseball, and we have that minor league team in Kalamazoo. We could go to a game.

Interviewer: That's a good starting point. You are a good father . . . you can get back there. Let's talk about any issues that could make that plan work or not work.

Client: Well, my energy level for one thing. And, I'd have to give up a night or two with my buddies at the bar.

Interviewer: Sounds like there would have to be some changes you would make. Would you like to discuss these issues? Because we would like this plan to be a success.

Client: No, I'm optimistic. I want my son back. We'll go to a game tonight.

Interviewer: Okay, things are stressful at home . . . the real stressor is your relationship with your son. Your wish is to go back to the time when you and your son were very close . . . you miss that. Your thought is to take him to a ballgame and see if that can start a better relationship.

Client: I hope it works. I think it will. My father never did anything with us. What do I do if he says "no"?

Interviewer: Then we work together and either adjust the plan or go to a new one. Remember, being a good father is important for you.

We now move into the client's issue of his relationship with his son. We will implement the skills designed for that issue and begin to move the client to the discovery of the role alcohol plays in his relationship with his son and in self-medicating the depressive disorder.

Session Five With George

Interviewer: Good to see you. How was this past week, and how did the plan go?

Client: Well, both good and bad.

Interviewer: A lot like life.

Client: I guess. We went to a ballgame on Tuesday night. It was a great game. We went to dinner first and talked baseball and stuff . . . it felt so good.

Interviewer: So, he didn't say "no."

Client: Right, he was excited. It was going well until the fifth inning of the game. I was getting thirsty. I went to the concession stand and got him a pop, and I bought a beer. When I got back to the seats, he saw the beer, and he didn't say a word to me the rest of the night. It was only one beer, I wasn't drunk. My drinking affects him, doesn't it? It ruined the whole night. I felt miserable—guilty, in your words. I knew it all along. I just didn't want to deal with it.

Interviewer: So, what happened after the game?

Client: I desperately needed a drink and to go to the bar to be with my buddies, but I used some of those skills you've been talking to me about. I tried the self-soothing stuff, but the big issue was I went to apologize to him. My drinking hurts him, just like it hurt me as a kid. I thought my alcohol didn't hurt my son because I never hit him, but it does hurt him. I've got to quit drinking, I've got to, but it scares me. We are going to another game tonight, and I promised him there would be no alcohol. I've been trying to cut back this week. I want my son back.

Interviewer: You want to be a good father. You want to change behaviors because of that. How have the attempts at cutting back been to you?

Client: Not well. I get really depressed and nervous when I go too long. I'm going to miss my friends at the bar and that energized feeling.

Interviewer: This will be a struggle. We'll work through this, because you are motivated. You want to be a good father.

He was placed in a dual-diagnosed enhanced detox program, which treated the depression with appropriate medical interventions. His therapy lasted nine months. At the writing of this book he has been sober for 19 years. His son received his master's degree in social work and now works as an addictions counselor. This case study appears in this book with their permission.

Commentary

Adherence to treatment and enduring abstinence and sobriety is our hope for our clients. As we know, however, from data and numbers commented on earlier, that wish often goes unfulfilled. But, with appropriate motivation that is focused on the discrepancy in the client's life, this goal and its acquisition is enhanced. In fact, some interesting studies emphasize the role of motivation in the self-medicating mentally ill. What is also of interest are the number of studies that validate the benefit of a process called adaptations of motivational interviewing (AMI; Heather, Rollnick, & Bell, 1992). This AMI frame is applied to interventions that incorporate additional non-motivational interviewing strategies while retaining the principles of motivational interviewing. What I have produced is a minor version of an AMI. It is an adaptation that appreciates and incorporates the basic principles of Miller and Rollnick's theory, but it takes a different track in the area of the discovery of the discrepancy. The bottom line is that nobody changes behaviors without motivation; how you get the client motivated can be a journey with varied paths.

Once the client discovers his discrepancy, our function and role as counselor changes. With the client moving toward motivation and a desire to change behaviors, then the counselor becomes an advisor. Some readers may be uncomfortable with the behavioral tone of that function. The point is to be flexible in your therapy relationship. However clinicians want to frame their role with motivated clients is pretty much up to them.

Now that the discrepancy has been discovered, it becomes the focus of our counseling. We want to remain attached to this discrepancy, because it will usually be correlated to the issue of resistance. In George's case, he gave me a gift when he began to express pain over the relationship with his son. It was vital to our relationship and his acquiring eventual motivation to change behaviors that I encouraged him to go there. It was also vital to our relationship that he go down this road on his own. Quite often we may feel the urge to prematurely point out to clients that their discrepancy is related to the drug and/or alcohol use. Remember, we do not instill motivation.

It was important for George to discover this correlation between his relationship with his son and his alcohol use on his own. I would have done great damage to our relationship—if not totally destroy it—if I had brought George to his knees in our first session with the following insight: "Of course you are having problems with your son; you're a drunk and it has been my experience that drunks have a serious challenge in raising kids." Say good-bye to any hope for a therapy relationship and to hoping George would develop any motivation to change. George would have walked away from that first session with an even stronger level of resistance than he had when he walked into our first session. Even a more subtle, less accusatory form of this confrontation ("George, have you ever considered that your use of alcohol may be one issue that is harming your relationship with your son?") could have done damage and further cemented his resistance.

The bottom line is that clients need to sense an ownership of the therapy process. They deserve the right to explore these possible correlations between their pain/discrepancy and their current resistance. When they do discover this correlation, as George eventually did, it is a personal discovery and not one that was handed to them. They, therefore, deserve the praise and accolades for this accomplishment and not having to thank the therapist for this wonderful insight. Therapy is a relationship and, in that understanding, clients should be allowed and encouraged to do as much work as the therapist. I often wonder if the dismal outcome studies that addiction counselors achieve may be due, in part, to our telling clients what to do and prematurely pointing out to them insights that they should be encouraged to discover; therefore, we do all the work and rob clients of a personal investment in their own recovery.

Although the therapist has now been given the gift in the dis-covered pain/discrepancy, we want to make sure that we spend just enough time to explore all of the aspects of this current condi-tion. I encouraged George to tell me about his history with his son. I wanted to know about his history with his own father. I wanted to know how he saw himself as a parent and how this current state of affairs with his son was damaging to his self-image and, there-fore, stimulating further alcohol use to self-medicate his emotions of worthlessness and failure. I was especially touched when he revealed to me the circumstances of the "promise." His father came home drunk and began to assault his mother. He stepped in and tried to protect his mother, and the father assaulted him viciously. While he was awaiting the ambulance to take him to the hospital, he promised himself: "If I am ever lucky enough to have children, I will never treat them like this. I will love my children." He was 13 years old when he made that promise. And now, at the time of his telling me this tale, his son walks out of the room when he walks in. This, dear reader, is a powerful discrepancy.

We do *not*, however, want to spend too much time on this discussion of pain/discrepancy. This is a vital place to visit, but we do not want our client to live there. When we sense that we have ample informa-tion about the pain/discrepancy, we move on. I can imagine that many of you have had experiences where your client is quite satisfied with staying here and discussing their hurt for way too long. Some stud-ies reveal that staying on this topic for a prolonged period can result in higher levels of depression and anxiety (Velasquez, Carbonari, & DiClemente, 1999).

Now the conversation should turn to the question of "What are we going to do about this problem?" At this time, clients are talking about a pain/discrepancy in their lives. We will be assisting them in the development of management of this pain. During this phase, clients will, hopefully, discover the correlation between their pain and the issue of their resistance. We will guide them to discover how the pain/discrepancy is actually strengthened by the issue of resistance.

What are we going to do about this problem—this identified discrepancy and locus of pain? George is ready to discuss plans to revitalize and recapture his relationship with his son. He has tried different things to achieve that goal, but all attempts have ended in failure. Again—and I stress this—we are not ignoring the issue of alcohol use in this dilemma. I was quite sure that George's alcohol use played a major role in this deteriorating relationship with his son, but he had to discover this issue. In order for his motivation for change to be enduring, he had to discover the role of alcohol in his life. George knew what did not work with his son. He now had to develop a plan that was acceptable to him, accessible, and would give him some hope of effectiveness. Therefore, George and I talked. We talked about various strategies that could effectively change the relationship he had with his son. George wanted to be closer to his son, but he did not know how to accomplish this goal. He had some thoughts, but they were just thoughts. He had not considered the complex nature of operationalizing those plans. In other words, George said he was ready and determined to change his relationship with his son, but he lacked the plans for doing so.

The task ahead was to use his motivation in making a solid and realistic assessment of the challenges he might encounter in moving closer to his son. I wanted him to think creatively about how to develop the plan that offered the best opportunity for success. I encouraged him to put everything on the table. I wanted him to consider the personal challenges—one of which was his use of alcohol—and his previous experiences in his relationship in the development of these change strategies. I asked him for permission to share some of my experiences as a father of five children. I asked him for permission to share strategies that I have heard from other parents in similar situations. Neither he nor I brought up the alcohol issue at this point. It was his responsibility and privilege to discover this issue.

When all this energy was harnessed and all the data collected, we created a menu of possible options to achieve his goal. We then began a process of choosing the option that offered the best opportunity for success. I did, on occasion, advise him against plans that appeared inappropriate or lacking in substance, such as "having a heart-to-heart talk." I had to remind him that we were talking about a 14-year-old teenager and not an adult. This was not an easy phase in our relationship. On more than one occasion, I fought within myself to avoid unilaterally mentioning the alcohol use. I had to respect his state of resistance on this issue, and, I believe, he respected me for that. This phase of planning for change is the guts of the therapy relationship. George did a lot of talking, and I did a lot of listening. We developed a relationship.

After our menu of change options was complete, we began the process of examining each option with what is often described as the pros and cons exercise. We wanted to look at each strategy to discover the behavioral and emotional variables that would either contribute to or detract from its success potential. It was at this time that the function and presence of alcohol—the "elephant in the room"—was brought up. George brought the subject to the conversation as a potential roadblock to success. It was here he began a challenging process of examining—slowly and with great hesitation—the role his drinking played in his relationship with his son. He knew that whatever plan we decided upon, there would have to be some changes made. He knew that his use of alcohol was one of them. He was not committing to sobriety at this point. He was merely becoming aware that to operationalize any of the plans, he would, in all probability, have to compromise—"give up a night with my buddies at the bar"—on his alcohol use. He was, however, motivated. He was willing to do what was necessary. Without this motivation, which flowed from his discrepancy/pain over the poor relationship with his son, he would have never accepted these "sacrifices." Finally, he decided on the plan to take his son to a ballgame, and this became the watershed event of his life.

When our clients begin to implement the plan of action designed to manage the discrepancy in their lives, this is where behavioral change becomes real. Up to this point, George and I were just talking. These conversations were vital, as he discovered the best way to reunite with his son. It was, however, just talk. This talk must be directed toward action. This action must be directed toward behavioral change. This phase is the most demanding on the counselor and the client. Behavioral change becomes visible and operationalized, along with missteps, impediments, starts and stops in motivation, and levels of commitment. There will be times where the plan needs modification. There are times where the original plan does not work and needs to be replaced with another approach. George took his son to the ballgame, and it was affirmed for him that his son did not care for his drinking: "It's the alcohol, isn't it?" He then began his arduous journey into sobriety. He took his son to another ballgame, and this time there was no alcohol. It was a brutal experience for George, but it was emotionally rewarding in the closeness he felt with his son that evening. After that event, it was determined that medically supervised detox was advisable. None of this would have ever happened if George had not been motivated.

During this time he still had conflicting feelings about sobriety. He missed his previous lifestyle. He also missed, most importantly, the benefits of alcohol use. Recall that all behaviors are purposeful. People do what they do for a reason, because this behavior—even dysfunctional and maladaptive behaviors—benefits them in some way. For George, his alcohol helped him manage his undetected depressive disorder and gave him social cohesion. He missed his drinking buddies (social cohesion) and that energized feeling (transient relief from co-occurring depression). Constant affirmation from me was essential at this point. George received all the praise and congratulations for his move to sobriety. With this move, however, came the threat of relapse. At this point, our clients need significant doses of self-efficacy. Without this self-efficacy, our clients are not likely to experience long-term, enduring abstinence and/or sobriety.

Relapse is not a failure; it is a teachable moment and a learning experience. Sustaining behavioral change can be a significant challenge. Continued motivation is essential during this period of early and/or sustained remission. Without proper motivation, there will surely be relapse. For the self-medicating mentally ill with co-occurring disorders, this motivation is designed to encourage them in their journey of abstinence/sobriety and to bolster their respect for the need to remain faithful to their medication program. George self-medicated his depression with alcohol. He began this process when he was 13 years old. For him to remain on his medication was an essential piece of his recovery. George was wise enough to know that going off his meds was a dangerous prelude to relapse into alcohol use.

We talked earlier in this book about the function of education about drug/alcohol use. We warned that education about "your brain on drugs" is never to be used for motivation. The reason is that education does not work to motivate clients to change behaviors, but education does have an essential role in the overall treatment of co-occurring disorders—at a certain time and place. During recovery is the time and place where we educate clients about the function of drugs/alcohol in their lives. Now they will listen to us, whereas, if we give this message prematurely (before the discrepancy is discovered), it could result in further strengthening their resistance.

Relapse is part of recovery. Shame and embarrassment have no role to play in the processing of a relapse experience. For the co-occurring population, a relapse is just not using drugs and/or alcohol; it is also going off prescribed drugs for the mental disorder. The issue we remain alert to, however, is when the relapse is coupled with a regression to an earlier stage of motivation or, possibly, back to resistance. We would then be confronted with the challenge of reenergizing the client's motivation through the stages just defined. Be reminded, however, that this recycling through the phases of motivation is not unusual. Many clients repeat this cycle many times before they achieve enduring abstinence or sobriety. Also, quite often, people who do relapse have a better chance of success during the next cycle (Shiffman, 1982). They often discover new or different ways to deal with previous behaviors. Also, they now have the confidence of partial success to build affirmation and self-efficacy.

Relapses occur for many different, individual reasons. Clients want from the therapist a way to make sense or understand the relapse event. This is the element that makes it essential to the therapy relationship. Relapse can teach both the client and the counselor. The essential message is that relapse is an opportunity to learn and not a failure.

CHAPTER FIVE

Case Conceptualization for Co-Occurring Disorders

Getting to Know the Person

In the previous chapter we discussed the essential task in therapy for people with co-occurring disorders—discovering their pain/discrepancy. We will now turn our attention to the method by which this goal is accomplished and how we proceed after the discrepancy is discovered. The discovery of the locus of the client's pain is accomplished, quite simply, by getting to know the client. This effort has been studied and theorized for decades. In all of the theories, however, one issue remains clear. Our getting to know the client is best accomplished by exercising a thorough and comprehensive case conceptualization. The case conceptualization is not an event. This knowledge is gained through a process of examining several essential aspects of the client's life, including his or her history, current stressors, strengths and deficiencies, self-evaluation and worldview, and short- and long-term goals, wishes, and dreams. It is also accomplished through the self-examination by the therapist of the preferred approach to therapy.

CASE CONCEPTUALIZATION FOR CO-OCCURRING DISORDERS

The case conceptualization is essential to effective therapy and the development of a thorough treatment plan. Donald Meichenbaum, that renowned psychologist who has shared with us his insights on co-occurring disorders, said: "A clinician without a case conceptualization is like the captain of a ship without a rudder . . . aimlessly floating about with little or no direction" (Meichenbaum, 2010). Harry Stack Sullivan, quoted extensively in previous chapters, said: "One of the first tasks of therapy is to ask the question 'Who is this person and how does he/she come to be here?'" (Sullivan, 1954). Theorists including Kuyken, Padesky, Dudley, Persons, Berman, and Meichenbaum have shared valuable insights on the construction of the case conceptualization. Among these theorists, however, are key commonalities that are essential tasks for a complete knowledge of the client and a discovery of how best to begin the therapy alliance.

IDENTIFY DEVELOPMENTAL, PRECIPITATING, AND MAINTAINING FACTORS THAT CONTRIBUTE TO MALADAPTIVE BEHAVIORS

Recall the story of Walter in Chapter 3. He had recently been released from a few months in county jail on a charge of domestic violence. He came into my practice by the mandate of his probation officer and was in a state of resistance. Also recall the wisdom of Harry Stack Sullivan, who cautions us that many people will bring into our setting behaviors that are historic, chronic, childhood defense mechanisms. Walter began our conversation by projecting blame for all of his problems onto his wife, totally denying any responsibility for his actions, rationalizing his behaviors, and, quite interestingly, claiming benefits to his current behaviors. Paying attention to this remarkable defensiveness is vital. Walter was telling me volumes about his childhood, his emotional and psychological development, and what contributed to his current maladaptive behaviors. All of this was gained in the first 15 minutes of our relationship, and I didn't have to ask him one question. Walter gave me an invitation—not his intention, I'm sure—to pursue his developmental history. I took him up on his offer. This defensiveness came from somewhere, and it was my guess that it came from the dark hollows of an emotional and physically abusive childhood.

Over time he revealed his story to me. Everyone has a story. Case conceptualization is the outcome of the therapist's organizing the client's story into useful, pertinent subject headings. The information I received from Walter that contributed to this body of knowledge was of extreme help. From a behavioral perspective, Walter had been taught to use aggressive strategies to gain control. He had no modeling, nor was he ever taught to value self-control. He had limited capacity for empathy. His father battered his mother regularly. His father and his mother battered him. From Walter's perspective, both parents used verbal and physical violence as their only child management strategy. Therefore, Walter learned to use aggression through modeling. He discovered at an early age—around seven or eight—that if he denied responsibility, projected blame, and rationalized behaviors, that he could, on occasion, deflect the battering. These behaviors became very important defenses for him to avoid emotional and physical punishment. He also discovered, at the age of 10, alcohol. Alcohol became his only mechanism to ward off personal feelings of worthlessness, self-devaluation, depression, and anxiety. He began to self-medicate. Now, here he is—three decades removed from this turmoil—with serious problems with his violent behavior, excessive drinking, and an inability to assume responsibility for his own behavior.

As we identify the developmental, precipitating, and maintaining factors that contribute to Walter's maladaptive behaviors, we are immediately struck by the faulty learning experiences his childhood provided. His parents modeled aggressive behaviors as problem-solving strategies and were woefully weak in demonstrating or encouraging socially appropriate behaviors. Walter learned that to be in control of interpersonal relationships, he had to be violent. This developmental learning experience taught him that when control was not in his grasp, violence was the antidote. The precipitating factor, therefore, was his individualized sense of powerlessness. Maintaining his use of violence during this feeling of inadequacy was the undeniable fact that, in some settings, the violence helped him regain a sense of command. Alcohol use had multifaceted benefits. Although he was a self-medicator, the alcohol also dulled the pain when he was not in control.

This material was essential for me to acquire. What is fascinating is that this knowledge was pursued after I received an invitation from the client in the form of his maladaptive defensiveness. All behaviors are purposeful. This defensiveness the client so willingly displayed for me came from somewhere. All I had to do was to prick him a bit with an open invitation to tell me his story, and he gladly complied.

The violence, however, had resulted in legal entanglements. All of the blaming and projecting and denying he could demonstrate was not going to change the fact that he was on probation. The alcohol use was also a factor in his being mandated to treatment. Violence and alcohol use—behaviors that kept him emotionally afloat and were essential for him to feel a sense of control—were now being seen as problematic. My hope is that in this dilemma lies his discrepancy. His lifelong coping and management strategies could now, possibly, be seen as detrimental to something he values—his freedom, autonomy, independence. This is a fragile discrepancy, but, at times, it is all we can get by on.

IDENTIFY INDIVIDUAL DEVELOPMENTAL PROTECTIVE FEATURES AND STRENGTHS

Ironically, Walter's need for freedom, autonomy, and independence is both a protective feature and a strength. It is a strength that the therapist is going to build on and emphasize during the therapy relationship. Unfortunately, Walter exercised this need for autonomy in a maladaptive fashion. During therapy the therapist offered him alternative methods to accomplish this admirable goal of feeling that he was in charge of his own life. The therapist began this process by emphasizing to the client his ability to make personal choices and be in control.

A source of Walter's resistance was his reaction to being mandated into therapy. This mandate of being told what to do triggered his lifelong defense mechanism of projection of blame and denying responsibility.

He reacted to this mandate by asserting his autonomy. This is a very common and natural reaction to a loss of liberty and autonomy. Although Walter's resistance was viewed as a psychological defense mechanism that was developed during childhood, what happened in the therapy alliance was determined by the therapist's response to the resistant behavior. Basically, if the therapist sees the resistance increasing during the relationship, it is likely this is a response to something the therapist is doing. Continued, persistent resistance in therapy is, therefore, reflective of the therapist's interaction style. What this essentially means is that we can assess our effectiveness by observing the client's decrease, or increase, in resistant behavior during the relationship. In Walter's case, therefore, I emphasized his capacity to make personal choices.

One essential strategy to decrease resistance and increase clients' productive involvement in therapy is to discover and bring into the therapy alliance their strengths. Everybody has strengths. For some clients we have to search for them. In Walter's case, one of his strengths, as mentioned, was his desire to be autonomous and in control of his own life. His understanding of this strength was to be in a position of "not being told what to do." I reframed that strength for him by emphasizing during our relationship his "need to be in control of his own life." I remained unflinching in reminding him, during the course of therapy, of that reframe. I consistently reminded him that if he decided to pursue sobriety (and it *is* his choice), this strength would be of vital importance. But what of other strengths that may have resided in the character of this troubled man?

Many people with co-occurring disorders are quite pessimistic, even hopeless, on the issue of recovery. They are often in desperate need of confidence. Clients may be motivated to change since they discovered their discrepancy. They may now see that current behaviors are preventing them from obtaining what they value and want in their lives—the discrepancy. They are ready and willing to change. They also need to view themselves as capable of pursuing abstinence/sobriety if they desire that outcome and see it necessary to obtain what they value and want in their lives. The essential path to instill confidence is to pursue with clients their strengths. For many

111

clients, these strengths may not be readily accessible or recognized. At times, the therapist has to bring them to their attention.

Clients may be motivated and see the importance of change, but unless that view is coupled with confidence, movement toward change may be a challenge. An issue of importance here, however, is to respect when clients' low level of confidence is the result of serious character issues of chronic depression, significant low self-esteem, or learned helplessness. These insidious issues, when discovered in therapy, may have to be addressed separately before a more behavioral approach to increasing confidence may be achieved.

As we go down the path of discovering strengths and instilling confidence, we learn to approach several issues cautiously and, if possible, avoid them. For instance, we need to avoid doing all the work and telling clients what they need to do to achieve what they value and want in their lives. Therapy is a reciprocal and mutual relationship. Clients are our partners on their road to recovery and *not* our students. Clients are not empty vessels that we fill with our wonderful wisdom about life. I have sadly found that the more I tell clients what they should do, that frame increases their desire to tell me what they can't do. There is no one-size-fits-all prescription to recovery. Although what works for one person may be helpful to another, the risk remains that it may not. We share our ideas with clients when we feel it is appropriate and when they are ready to hear them.

Another style to be cautious of in the road to confidence is being a cheerleader and believing that pep talks are all clients need to boost their energy. That approach may be viewed by clients as seriously lacking empathy for their lack of confidence. We may present to clients a sense of not getting it when we try to superficially make them feel confident. We run a risk here of not taking the issue of lack of confidence seriously enough.

Finally, it is important that we avoid becoming pessimistic ourselves when confronted with the challenge of leading people with co-occurring disorders to recovery. It may be the most significant risk. It has been mentioned before in this text that these people may be the most significantly challenging population we meet in our careers. It is vital that we remain steadfastly hopeful about their recovery.

We also need to instill that hopeful attitude for our clients. We will never quit on them. They may relapse, seem hopeless, fail to appear for sessions, or may present with therapy-interfering behaviors, but we remain with them. Our clients may never achieve our hopes for them, but we remain with them. There may be times when we will not be able to assist our clients in achieving abstinence/sobriety. We may, on occasion, only move our clients to reducing the harm that their use of drugs creates. They may continue to use alcohol/drugs, but in a fashion that creates less havoc in their lives. Our clients are important people, and we will be there when they need us.

What are some strategies to enhance confidence and discover strengths? One method is to begin by eliciting clients' thoughts on the subject of change. Remember, clients are motivated to change—they have discovered their discrepancy. They probably have given some thought to this issue. The therapist needs to know what those thoughts are. We accept and affirm their thoughts and ideas and, if appropriate, build on them. When we build on them, however, remember the cautions mentioned in this chapter. We often ask permission before engaging in the embellishment of clients' ideas. We give advice when clients are either ready for it or ask for it.

The therapist also wants to look at previous attempts to achieve abstinence/sobriety and the lessons those attempts have revealed. We would also want to explore any changes clients have made in their lives and the specific aspects of those occasions. Therefore, reviewing past successes at changing behaviors is an excellent method of identifying strengths, enhancing confidence, and offering affirmation to clients. The issue we want to discover here is times when the client self-initiated some behavioral change. We want to explore these efforts in detail, with special attention paid to identifying strengths. When we do identify a strength, we would then want to generalize that issue and apply it to the current motivation to change behaviors. Remember also that when these strengths are brought to attention, clients are given affirmation.

At times we have to pay very close attention to clients' stories in order to clearly recognize and bring attention to a strength. As an example I want to recapture what Walter told me about his one previous attempt at sobriety. The event occurred many years before I met him and represented his first mandated counseling. He had just received his second DUI and was mandated by the court into therapy. He continued to drink while on probationary status, although he was under abstinence-mandated court supervision. He attended his first session, as directed, and was immediately asked by the counselor if he was maintaining his abstinence. Walter reported to me that he told the counselor that he had not been abstinent, and he told the counselor the reasons for his drinking—to self-calm during periods of dysregulated anxiety and rage. The counselor was not happy and reported him immediately to the court. The court, in turn, gave Walter a three-month jail term for violations of the court order. I told Walter, as he concluded the story, that I was very impressed with his honesty. When the counselor asked about his sobriety, he was honest and reported that he had been drinking. He could have lied. He was truthful and paid the price. I was impressed. I wanted to bring attention to and affirm this strength. This affirmation and this attribute of honesty were major contributions for Walter and I having a productive counseling relationship.

IDENTIFY SHORT-TERM AND LONG-TERM GOALS

This construct in the case conceptualization is the essential component for the formulation of the treatment plan. As I get to know clients, a discovery of what they desire in life and what their goals are for therapy are the key features. Treatment plans are pathways to goal attainment. The treatment plan gives the clients and the therapist a sense of direction. The goals to be obtained often depend on clients' capacity to identify the locus of their pain. When this hurt and pain is uncovered in therapy, it becomes the focus of the long-term goal. Long-term goals, essentially, are ambitious and comprehensive goals that stem from and are generated by the pain/discrepancy in a person's life.

The short-term goals are focused on helping clients learn skills so that this pain/discrepancy may be better managed. The short-term goals will be, therefore, brief, specific, measurable management strategies that move clients toward obtaining the long-term goal (managing the pain/discrepancy). Short-term goals should be clearly defined and obtainable in order to instill hope for clients. These short-term goals are often complex. In the case of George, discussed earlier in this work, he discovered that his pain/discrepancy was his relationship with his son. His long-term goal, therefore, was to repair and enhance his parenting and, through that, reestablish his relationship with his son. The short-term goals that were established were designed to help George obtain that goal. We measure our effectiveness in treatment by documenting our clients' attainment of these behaviorally measured goals. Short-term goals take advantage of strengths and respect maladaptive features that could be therapy-interfering behaviors.

The major strength that George provided—and that became a major influence in the development of our goals—was his love for his son. Also, the defined short-term goals depend on the client's input. Does the client see the short-term goals as reasonable, pertinent, relevant, obtainable, realistic, and consistent with the client's views of the pain/discrepancy? Because of this, George initially did not identify sobriety as a short-term goal that was needed to enhance his parenting and improve his relationship with his son. It was only after he discovered the role of alcohol in the deteriorating relationship that he included sobriety in his short-term goals. It is vital, when developing short-term goals, to take the big picture with clients and become as comprehensive as possible.

We remain sensitive to the complexity of our clients' lives and never try to simplify their pain or attempt to simplify the pathway to manage that pain. George's short-term goal arrangement expanded significantly as he began to get a realistic sense of the enormity of this challenge ahead of him. For instance, once he agreed that alcohol use played a major role in his relationship with his son and sobriety became a short-term goal, his outlook became more threatened and pessimistic because of the numerous complications in the issue of sobriety. The complexity of the short-term goals began to threaten his motivation to obtain the long-term goal. His strength—his love for his son—allowed us to prevail during this rather tenuous period in therapy.

An example of the short-term goals that George approached and achieved during his quest for sobriety could, perhaps, help in operationalizing this concept. The first goal was to teach George to be mindful of himself as an individual in recovery. I wanted to teach him skills for how to pay attention to himself and the world in which he lived. These skills would be essential for him to sustain his sobriety and, therefore, enhance his relationship with his son. He needed to become mindful so as to respect his periods of yearning for his drug. He needed to respect and learn of the temporary nature of these cravings. He needed to be aware of his physical and emotional reactions to these yearnings in order to effectively manage them. He needed to learn his triggers and vulnerabilities and those times when alcohol use was so attractive to him. I remember starting this process by asking him to visit a local mall and spend an hour at that location with the purpose of watching for an act of human kindness. Initially, he felt this was foolish, but as he was very motivated by the love for his son, he agreed. After a few mindfulness exercises, he became engrossed in this process and began a weekly chart of his mindfulness experiences.

Another short-term goal that was essential to address was his feeling about the unfairness of his life, especially his addiction. He did not aspire to become addicted to alcohol. When he first experienced alcohol at the age of 13, his goal was not to become an alcohol-addicted person. His goal was to become the life of the party. His goal was to become popular with his peers and to get some temporary relief from his dysthymia. His addiction was a tragic outcome to a behavior that started for a very understandable purpose, but now he was addicted. The fairness or unfairness of life has little room in the therapy alliance and makes a very inappropriate goal. We cannot change nature. He was not going to transform into a social drinker. Sobriety was going to be a lifelong challenge. We coached him into accepting that life is what it is. This radical acceptance of life permitted him to manage the periodic stressors of being a person in recovery. This acceptance is taught in the relationship with our clients. We teach them by our acceptance of them and the condition they bring to us that they are who they are.

A third short-term goal is the acquisition of emotional regulation skills. The period of recovery is laden with emotional turmoil. The clients' world should not have to compromise and accept emotional dysregulation from the person in recovery. It is the clients' responsibility to learn how to self-regulate and self-soothe these emotions that had been calmed by drug use. George began to experience periodic spikes in unregulated anger. Usually, a few drinks would help calm him down. During sobriety he had to accomplish this task without his drug. He began, at this time, to discover the multifaceted benefit that alcohol provided for him. He also really began to miss his "best friend." Relapse was painfully close. Now was the time to teach him how to regulate these emotions without alcohol. An example was Linehan's "opposite to emotion skill" (Linehan, 1999). He began a process of singing a tune from his favorite musical during spikes in emotion. He discovered, rather humorously, that when he sang these tunes, the anger spike was modified and had lessened impact on his social and relational functioning. He began to learn that when he acted in a way that was different from the way he was feeling, that these emotions, with potentially maladaptive consequences, were manageable.

George also discovered, during this time, photography. He found a way to have pleasure without alcohol. He discovered with his mindfulness skills that photography of nature provided him with the same soothing and calmness that alcohol had achieved. Photography became, for a while, his new medication, and he became addicted to the process of taking pictures of trees. This newfound source of pleasure was essential. George had to discover another way to find pleasure and another passion. Much of his attention was placed on his son. That was, however, a rather unfair burden to place on a 14-year-old boy. George had to find his own personal passion.

Finally, his friends at the bar. What about them? George "bonded through Budweiser." Most of his life friendships were focused on alcohol use. This was his greatest challenge. George, by nature, was not graced with social skills. His alcohol use opened the door for him to have a social environment. Once again, he could not rely on his son to become his best buddy. That is unfair. George accepted the fact that he would have fewer friends. He believed, for a while, that his bar buddies would "hang in with him," but they drifted off gradually, and he became alone. This was a brutal time for him. It reminded him of his childhood and the reason he started drinking in the first place. We taught him, therefore, interpersonal relationship skills. These skills were taught in the relationship I had with this wonderful man. When we were angry at each other, we expressed this emotion. We expressed feelings in our professional relationship that were similar to his experiences at the bar. He did make a few friends.

Strategies for Obtaining Important Information

1. *Gather information about childhood experiences.* The therapist is interested in gaining information from clients about childhood events that may have played a role in the eventual development of their self-image. Joseph Sabbath comes to mind, again, as he tells us repeatedly: "The tragedy of child abuse is that the abused child incorporates the identity given to them by the predator" (Sabbath, 1969). Listen to clients tell their stories and attend to any elements that you feel may have shaped the manner in which they identify themselves. These messages may not have been traumatic. They may, however, have had a major impact in the formulation of the clients' worldview. They may, for instance, come from homes where alcohol was used in a nonproblematic fashion, and the message given by this use is that being intoxicated is fun, or people like you better when you are drunk, or intoxication can lead to love or creativity. They may, however, have lived in homes where the use of drugs was extremely harmful, hurtful, and destructive, and the message on the self-image may be of significant self-hate and/or self-devaluation.

2. *Explore current life stressors.* This is taking the big picture of the world in which clients live. This world, by the way, may not be anywhere near your world. Attention in treatment needs to focus on unemployment, health issues, relationship turmoil, legal problems, housing challenges, financial crises, and psychiatric

concerns. Therapists also need to attend to what issues brought clients to their attention. If clients were mandated to therapy, we may discover very low motivation and high resistance. We also need to discover their history of treatment. Was the treatment efficacious, did they adhere to counseling, were they satisfied with the therapy relationship? Do they have an extensive treatment history marked by pronounced relapses? If so, are they feeling hopeless regarding sobriety/abstinence?

3. *Ask when and why clients began using drugs/alcohol.* This is an essential component in the case conceptualization of people with co-occurring disorders. The therapist is seeking to discover the benefit of drug/alcohol use for clients. This focus begins with the query: "Can you give me a history of your substance use?" The therapist will be paying very close attention to the metaphors the clients use as they detail their history of drug use. Such metaphors as "When I'm drunk, I'm the life of the party" or "When I'm stoned, I don't have a worry in the world" can give us a lead that these clients are self-medicating an undetected, untreated mental disorder. This information may also lead us to discover these clients' vulnerability to drug use — when they experience a heightened level of symptoms. The therapist wants to discover all of the aspects of the clients' initial experience with drugs/alcohol. We want to know the social, emotional, relational, economic, occupational dynamics that may have played a role in the initial drug/alcohol experiment.

4. *Explore how clients became dependent and the realization that they could not stop on their own.* Obviously, not all drug/alcohol users become addicted. As a matter of record, only a small percentage of drug/alcohol users eventually experience addiction. The key here is, however, that addiction is a tragic consequence to a behavior that began for a beneficial reason — a purpose. In my career of nearly five decades, I have never met an individual who has proclaimed to me that when they began their use of drugs/alcohol, the stated goal was to become an addict. This has never happened to me; nor will it ever happen. Drug/alcohol use begins for a reason, and, at times, that reason is to provide transient,

temporary relief from the symptoms of an undiagnosed and untreated mental illness. We need to emphasize this point to our clients. We need to impress upon them that they began the use of drugs for an attractive reason. We then need to discover with clients the circumstances in which they began to experience the first markers of dependency—withdrawal, using more of the drug, frenzied attempts to acquire the drug. And we also need to discover with the clients: "Why them?" Out of the tens of millions of substance users in society, what particular issues may have made this client vulnerable to addiction?

5. *Determine how clients functioned prior to their use of drugs.* As we visit, or revisit, this history we will be looking for the conditions that made clients vulnerable to drug use. As we emphasize this past, we are also discovering that those issues may still create this vulnerability. Another benefit is that the exploration of this history may yield some information on the discrepancy that we so vitally need for a successful therapy experience. The therapist will examine clients' educational, vocational, relational, and social history. We want to view clients through different developmental stages that were the pathways to drug use.

6. *Discover the diagnostic profile.* It is essential for the therapist to formulate a diagnostic framework for clients. This framework enhances our understanding of clients and the accuracy and relevance of our treatment plan. In order to develop this framework, the therapist needs a working knowledge of the new, expanded, and contracted diagnostics in DSM-5. For example, due to expanded diagnostics in the DSM-5, many more citizens will qualify for the diagnosis of PTSD. There is, as mentioned earlier in this book, a powerful correlation between PTSD and alcohol and cannabis use for self-medicating purposes. The DSM-5 presents a greater challenge in the diagnosis of people with personality disorders. The process is going to be much more complex and comprehensive and accurate. The diagnosing of a client with a personality disorder, while challenging, will be essential to recognize the function and role character issues have in therapy and in the quest for sobriety/abstinence. There

are other changes coming in this marvelous work, which are too numerous and complex to address in this book.

7. *Determine implications for the therapy alliance.* The implications for the case conceptualization are numerous, complex, and profound. First, it should begin to answer the question: Is this client appropriate for this therapist's style of therapy? Some of us are behaviorists; some more psychodynamic. Some therapists rely on interpersonal relationships in therapy to teach new skills. Some therapists are integrationists. Whatever the style is, we must never try to fit the client into our therapy approach. If the client does not fit, then we would be ethically motivated to find a counselor with whom the client would fit. Some people are not suited for insight-oriented therapy. Some citizens may not be capable of responding to cognitive-behavioral approaches. We discover this issue during the case conceptualization and respond accordingly. The other benefits and implications on the therapy alliance include a discovery of the client's individual personality characteristics; a discovery of the client's discrepancy, motivation to change, and goals; a discovery of potential therapy-interfering behaviors; and, finally, a discovery of the therapist's realistic goals for this client at this time.

CASE CONCEPTUALIZATION FROM A MODEL FOR CO-OCCURRING DISORDERS

We talked earlier about the terminology used to classify and describe people who self-medicate a mental illness with drugs and/or alcohol. The term *co-occurring disorders* replaced the terms *dual disorders* or *dual diagnosed* to describe and classify this population. The latter terms were seen as confusing because they often referred to people who had a developmental disability and a mental illness. Furthermore, these latter terms suggest that only two disorders are co-occurring when, in fact, there may be more. People with co-occurring disorders may have multiple, complex issues in their lives that may display varying degrees of severity and disability. A diagnosis of co-occurring disorders is made when at least one disorder of each category (cocaine dependency and schizophrenia) can be established independent of the other and cannot be explained as a group of symptoms resulting from one disorder (alcohol-induced depression caused by withdrawal).

The combinations of co-occurring drug disorder problems and psychiatric disorders differ in many realms. These problem combinations vary in areas such as severity, disability, chronicity, and degree of impairment in functioning. For example, the two defined disorders may both be mild or, in some instances, one may be mild and the other may present as severe. Both may display different levels of disability and/or impairment in specific areas of functioning. Also, the severity of the disorders may change over time and need periodic reclassification. Therefore, there is a challenge in defining and classifying the varied complexities that people with co-occurring disorders present. In the effort toward case conceptualization, this challenge is unique.

Kenneth Minkoff, MD, provides a unique way to offer a case conceptualization framework to this population. He presents a model where this population is divided into four groups (or quadrants) based on levels of severity for the substance use and the mental illness. He further guides us in appropriate treatment approaches for each of the four quadrants. Let's describe the four quadrants that Dr. Minkoff uses to offer a case conceptualization for co-occurring disorders:

Quadrant I: Low-severity mental illness/Low-severity substance use. Examples: A married man in his mid-forties with dysthymia. Is experiencing insomnia and some anxiety. Problems in marriage and job stress are pronounced. Discusses increased use of alcohol to sleep and avoid the anxiety due to job and marital stress.

Quadrant II: Severe persistent mental illness/Low-severity substance use. Examples: Man in his early forties with schizophrenia spectrum disorder. He lives in a residential program in the community sponsored by the local Community Mental Health Board. When he has access to it, he will consume a six-pack of beer on the weekends. He reports that he enjoys the use of alcohol, it allows him to "feel normal," but his fellow residents complain that he "gets loud" when using it.

Quadrant III: Low-severity psychiatric disorder/High-severity substance use with physiological dependence. Examples: A woman in her mid-thirties, engaged in prostitution, suffering symptoms of complex PTSD with depression (dysthymia). Severe issue of cocaine use with physiological dependency. She exchanges her sexual favors for access to drugs. She currently is on probation and has a lifelong history of trauma.

Quadrant IV/A: Severe persistent mental illness/High-severity substance use with physiological dependence. Examples: A woman in her late twenties with a diagnosis of Attenuated Psychotic Disorder. Severe issues of crack/cocaine use with physiological dependence and cannabis use with physiological dependence. She is homeless, living on the streets, involved in prostitution.

Quadrant IV/B: High-severity personality disorder driven maladaptive behaviors/High-severity substance use with physiological dependence. Examples: Woman in her mid-forties demonstrating behaviors associated with Borderline Personality Disorder (severe emotional dysregulation, poor interpersonal relationship skills, limited tolerance for stress, self-mutilates) with severe alcohol use with physiological dependence. Has long history of multiple detox admissions for alcohol, multiple inpatient psychiatric episodes, and multiple emergency room visits for suicidal behavior.

In Chapter 7 we explore and examine treatment principles that stem from these case conceptualization guidelines offered by Dr. Minkoff. For many decades, theorists have searched for the essential elements to therapy that have been related to positive treatment outcomes. What has been discovered? First, a respect that our clients are complex people is seen as essential for the therapy experience to be rewarding. The sooner we respect that principle, the sooner we move away from treating behaviors and move toward getting to know these complex, multifaceted people. Case conceptualizations give us a framework for that important task.

Also, we need to respect that therapy is a process and not an event. There is no clear-cut truth about our clients. As we explore them further, we gain insight into them and their world. Once again, case conceptualization gives us a model for that exploration. We wish to encourage our clients to be insightful about themselves and their world. Insight that has been specifically tied to the clients' concerns has been positively correlated to positive outcomes in therapy (Whiston & Sexton, 1993).

Finally, it has been repeatedly shown that the most important variable tied to a successful therapy experience was the relationship forged between the client and therapist (Grencavage & Norcross, 1990). It has been shown that whichever theoretical perspective a clinician takes, the genuine warmth and caring shown by the clinician ensures a productive relationship. Once again, a thorough case conceptualization assists in that process.

CHAPTER SIX

Suicide Risk Assessment for Co-Occurring Disorders

Before I begin this chapter on the exploration of suicide, I believe it is important to emphasize some of the issues that are involved in understanding this special population. No work on suicide is complete without respecting the essential contribution of Edwin Shneidman. Dr. Shneidman will be quoted extensively in this chapter, largely because of his extensive contribution to our knowledge of this issue. He is the one person whose insights into self-harm behaviors have given us the opportunity to understand, and sometimes prevent, this ultimate tragedy.

It is the stated goal of this chapter for the reader to gain respect for the *person* who is experiencing a suicidal episode. We emphasized in previous chapters the importance of treating the person and not the behaviors. Unfortunately, it is all too easy to lose track of this concept in working with the suicidal population. We become engrossed in lethality assessments, risk assessments, safety plans, and other such vehicles that place entirely too much emphasis on the behavior and miss the point of *why* this person is experiencing a suicidal crisis in the first place. Shneidman (1994) wrote, "The first task of therapy is to discover the locus of the client's unbearable pain and to decrease the hurt associated with that condition." Asking our clients "Where do you hurt?" will often reveal to us the focus of the suicide intent. People do what they do for a reason; all behaviors are purposeful. Suicide is a purpose-driven behavior designed to either eliminate or manage unbearable levels of psychological, emotional, and/or physical pain in their current life circumstances. Therefore, our clients often view suicide as a very attractive option that is seen as helpful and beneficial. Often, we view suicide as a dysfunctional or maladaptive behavior. Our clients, however, have a different perspective. We must develop an empathic approach to our clients' framework of suicide. Suicide is often their only option to manage pain. It is our endeavor, therefore, in the context of a caring relationship, to assist our clients in the discovery of their pain and to provide them with alternatives — as Shneidman said, "removing their blinders"—for solving and managing these issues in their lives. This chapter will explore that goal.

An essential theme that will be repeated throughout this chapter is: *Suicide is the ultimate individualized experience.* Edwin Shneidman commented years ago at a conference I was attending that "you can have a hundred suicidal folks in a room, and for each one of those people there will be a different pathway to suicide." Shneidman continuously reminded us that our clients' unbearable pain is "individually defined." He reminds us that "one person's unbearable agony is another person's irksome event." There is no universal definition of the suicide event. It is an event specific to each individual. That being said, let us now examine some of the common risk factors that studies have revealed are experienced by individuals early in the suicide process. Such an examination of risk factors to suicide is essential. These conditions create in a person a vulnerability to see suicide as an attractive problem-solving strategy. They are often called early suicide detectors and distal warning signs. The essential point here is that this is the clinician's point of intervention. Early intervention is the key, and these markers are the clinician's signal for early intervention. When these risk factors are observed in a clinical setting, the therapist is urged to pursue a gentle, respectful probing into the patient's possible suicidal thoughts.

The first two chapters strongly emphasized the fact that certain mental disorders are powerful correlates to co-occurring disorders. Depressive disorders (dysthymia and major depression) create powerful vulnerabilities, for example, for people to engage in drug use (alcohol, cocaine, opioids). They discover that when they are under the influence of certain drugs, they receive transient relief from the symptoms of these conditions. They find that certain drugs provide them with energy, enthusiasm, and passion. They become social, they become creative, and they ultimately enjoy life more when they are under the influence of drugs. They become the self-medicating mentally ill. They become people with co-occurring mental illness and substance-related (addiction) disorders. They have a condition that is a major correlate to completed suicide.

Studies by Klerman (1987), Minkoff and Regner (1999), and Meichenbaum (2010) reveal that "the interaction of substance use and depressive disorders is an especially lethal combination." Cornelius, Salloum, and Mezzich (1995) found that suicide was more common in patients with co-occurring depression and alcohol dependence when compared to patients with either disorder alone. The essential question we must ask of all people with substance-related (addiction) disorders is: "What does the drug do for you?" Listen to their responses and pay close attention to any metaphor giving a sense of the drug being used for relief from the symptoms of a mental disorder.

People with generalized anxiety disorders often self-medicate with cannabis. People with PTSD often self-medicate with alcohol and cannabis. People with bipolar I disorder often self-medicate with meth. People with psychotic disorders (schizophrenia) often self-medicate with alcohol, cocaine, and cannabis. David Clark, from Rush Hospital in Chicago, claimed: "Suicide rarely, if ever, occurs outside of the context of a major mental disorder" (Clark & Fawcett, 1992). Studies on completed suicides in any given year reveal that 90%, 93%, and 95% experienced at the time of their death a depressive disorder, bipolar disorder, anxiety disorder, or a psychotic disorder that was more often than not complicated by a co-occurring addiction disorder (Meichenbaum, 2010). The findings are obvious. Co-occurring disorders are lethal. The fact that your client is self-medicating puts that person at risk for premature, self-inflicted death.

These people often cannot see their lives without their drug. Their entire realm of functioning involves the acquisition and use of drugs. Vocational, occupational, relational, or social activities are secondary to, or are incorporated into, their pursuit of drugs. They will present in therapy behavioral criteria, which will qualify them for the DSM-5 diagnosis of Substance Use Disorder with Physiological Dependence. They are addicted. That condition, however, was not what they wanted or expected out of life. No one aspires to be an addict. Their use of drugs began to self-medicate, and the addiction was a tragic consequence of that purpose-driven activity. I have often found that while they continue to self-medicate, they also continue drug use for another purpose. They use their drugs to avoid the symptoms of withdrawal. I remember a young man telling me once during a session: "Telling me to quit cocaine is like telling me to quit breathing." The drug became essential for him to continue functioning.

These people are often involved in the criminal justice system when their history of use has resulted in social, relational, vocational, or occupational disasters. These patients frequently present in treatment by mandate and under coercion. They appear in a stage of resistance. Their risk for suicide is significant because of their vulnerability to hopelessness. Their view is that the only way out of this "living hell" they have found themselves in is to die.

What are some of the specific markers associated with completed suicide in this population? They experienced significant childhood pathology. Their history of drug use has resulted in significant losses in relationships, vocational and occupational opportunities, deteriorating physical health, financial challenges, and involvement in the justice system, and significant damage to self-esteem. They have a lessened sense of autonomy (literally becoming prisoners of their drug use) and display high levels of self-criticism and self-hate. Studies have added additional markers: history of poly-substance dependence, significant elements of sociopathy, callous disregard for the feelings of others, multiple treatment failures, history of multiple relapses, significant history of familial drug use, often coming from broken homes and victims of physical and/or emotional abuse as children (Murphy et al., 1988). My own experience with this population is wrought with alarm and concern. I have experienced many clients who were at risk for suicide in my 46-year career, but none are more at risk than the dually diagnosed patients at the extreme end of this spectrum. This is the realm of the hopeless addict.

PSYCHOLOGICAL VULNERABILITIES

Not all people with co-occurring disorders are at risk for suicide. Actually, only a small percentage of this population is at risk. In 1971 Edwin Shneidman asked a fascinating question: "The question of suicide is not why suicide; the question is, actually, why only some suicides?" When we look at the prevalence of the risk factors for suicide in this population, we are impressed by the data revealing that thousands of people with co-occurring disorders experience these markers. We lose only a fraction of them to suicide. Why them? That is often the question asked, and it is answered by examining deficiencies in coping and problem-solving skills. Shneidman notes that "all suicides are marked by a life-long pattern of weak, faulty coping and problem-solving skills" (Shneidman, 1971). We want to examine this issue as we discuss the psychological vulnerabilities that create a risk for suicide in certain populations. We approach these vulnerabilities from three areas: performance anxiety, emotional constriction, and the defenseless personality. Each of these conditions significantly weakens an individual's capacity to cope with stressors and to solve life's challenges.

Performance Anxiety

We all desire a sense of unconditional love in relationships. Most of us experience this during childhood. We receive rather constant messages, integrated into our relationships with our primary caregivers, that we are loved "because we exist." This allows a sense, as John Bowlby claimed in 1988, of having a "secure base." We are loved because we are lovable. This love will never be taken from us, it is secure, and we cannot lose it. Some of our clients, however, did not experience this love. Their experience was often tied to some expectation of performance. They experienced conditional affirmation and love. This message of love is not secure, and it gives the message that love is not freely given, it is quite fragile, and it can be lost. As long as these children perform according to expectations, they will receive affirmation and messages of love and regard. If they, however, fail to respond to their primary caregivers' expectations, that love and affirmation may be taken from them and replaced by messages of rejection.

From studies on suicide in gay, lesbian, bisexual, and transgendered adolescents, we know that these tragedies are significantly correlated to rejection and abandonment messages from primary caregivers when the adolescents "come out" in their sexual orientation. The issue in this personality frame is an inability to cope with and manage messages of failure. Failure experiences for this population are often translated as personal rejection and abandonment and a loss of love. Instead of a temporary blip on the screen of life, these failure experiences become instigators of a suicide desire. When people have a secure base, a failure experience results in a temporary emotional pain, but it does not become life threatening.

I met a client many years ago who, very sadly, met this criteria all too well. She was in her twenties and self-referred because of a "problem with alcohol." She was quite open about her history, which was heavily laden with performance messages from her parents. She was born into a home of high achievers, and as the youngest of four children, she was the only child not to meet the high expectations in this setting. She was a "great disappointment" to her parents, and her life was consistently aimed at eventually receiving their approval and love. The only way she could accomplish this was to engage in a vocational pursuit that was unattractive and "boring" to her. She managed the pain of these constant messages of failure and rejection with alcohol. She claimed once that intoxication was the only way she could deal with her family. She also claimed that "the only thing I am good at is getting drunk," "all I want is to be loved for who I am," and "when I am drunk I can turn off the TV of my life."

Alcohol became her coping strategy for feelings of failure and abandonment. Actually, alcohol was sustaining her and killing her simultaneously. Sobriety meant that she would have to manage her feelings of failure in other, less damaging, ways. This was frightening to her. She claimed during one of our early sessions that alcohol use was her "only way to cope" with her multiple, chronic feelings of abandonment. Alcohol had become her "best friend." She believed that sobriety could lead her to "off myself."

Emotional Constriction

"You know," the young man in my office said to me, "I used to be proud of the fact that nothing I see bothers me anymore. I've been a cop for over twenty years and I've seen everything. I used to brag about it. Nothing affects me. I had to do this to do my job. You can't be a cop and feel. But I think this is killing me. I'm dead inside. I can't feel anything." A week before I saw him, he was discovered by a fellow officer sitting at his locker with his revolver in his mouth. He was divorced, estranged from his two kids, living alone, no social context, and alcohol dependent. His only friends were the folks he hung out with at the bar. He "bonded through Budweiser." When he was intoxicated, he became social, talkative, and humorous, and he was free, temporarily, from this "dead inside" feeling. His use of alcohol was, literally, keeping him alive. His alcohol use gave him temporary relief from his dysthymia and also provided him with access to emotions that allowed him to stay alive.

"You know," he went on to say, "people like me better when I'm drunk. I'm actually a pretty funny guy . . . when I'm drunk. My ex-wife used to complain that the only time I would tell her I loved her was when I was drunk. And, you know, she was right." He looked as if he wanted to cry. I reflected my observation to him. I received a blank stare in response. He told me about his "jumpstart breakfast" — two fingers neat of Jim Beam with a Budweiser chaser. This was his morning medication that allowed him to function during the day. He told me that his first destination after his shift was the bar. It was his safe haven. It was there that he "debriefed" and "cleansed my soul." Alcohol made him emotionally available.

His story was sad. He had chosen a profession that required suspension of emotions. Many professions require this emotional shutdown.

These people are in professions where they are exposed to trauma—law enforcement, military, ER physicians and nurses, oncologists, EMS personnel, just to name a few. The only way they can discharge their duty is to shut down emotionally. After a while of this practice, it solidifies in the personality and becomes part of their functioning. This young man witnessed significant trauma on his job. He discovered that the only way to protect himself from the emotional onslaught of what he saw every day was to disconnect emotionally. He had to do this to do his job, but what was initially designed as a way to cope with his occupational demands now became a pervasive element of his personality. He became emotionally constricted. He lost his capacity to experience emotional reactions.

I remember during the initial stages of our relationship I asked him how a certain event impacted him from an emotional perspective. "How did that make you feel?" I asked him. His response to that question was a blank stare. I started reflecting emotions. "It must have been heartbreaking to see that," I offered. His response was a blank stare. Finally, I shared, as a model for this process, my own emotional reactions to his stories. "Something like that would make me quite angry," I offered. His response, again, was a blank stare. Without this capacity to be emotionally available, he began to lose relationships. It is difficult to develop and retain intimate relationships if you are not emotionally available. He became more and more alone. He became a person who self-medicated his depression, his aloneness, and his emotional constriction. All of these conditions intertwined in a lethal configuration. He became seriously vulnerable to completed suicide.

This client was emotionally constricted because of the demands of his profession. Many people are emotionally constricted because of developmental, childhood experiences of "emotional invalidation" (Linehan, Armstrong, Suarez, & Allmon, 1991). Sometimes these invalidating messages we give to our children are subtle: "Quit crying or I will give you something to cry about"; "wipe that smile off your face"; "that's no reason to get angry." And, quite often, these invalidating messages are pathological. These people are victims of childhood trauma—physical and sexual abuse. One of the more significantly damaging messages of abuse is: "I don't care how you feel; I'm going to do to you what I want to do to you. You can scream and cry all you want; I'm not going to stop. Your emotions are useless." The result of this tragedy is emotional constriction because emotional displays are useless. The person believes that "Nobody cares. Nobody knows how I feel. I am alone."

The Defenseless Personality

Edwin Shneidman made a comment years ago that "suicide is self-murder." And then he went on to say: "One cannot kill what one loves; one can only kill what one hates." This self-hate may be a temporary flash or a pervasive element of the self. The bottom line, however, is that these people believe they are not capable of solving life's problems and they are inadequate to effectively manage the pain in their lives. They feel, at the very least, helpless. And, at the extreme end of this spectrum, they are awash with self-hate and self-loathing.

I met a young woman many years ago who was on an internship at my practice as she pursued an advanced degree. She was brilliant. She was also a marvelous diagnostician and a wonderful therapist. She was going to be a gift to our profession. She accepted constructive direction and feedback very well. I noticed, however, that she did not take praise and affirmation very well. When I would point out some excellent work she was doing with a client, she would deflect my comments with self-depreciating humor. She would minimize the brilliance of her therapy strategies. She would reduce a wonderfully framed case conceptualization into a flash of luck. On one occasion, when I was stressing a marvelous therapy advance on her part, she actually cringed. Finally, I brought my observations to her attention. She acknowledged that it was characteristic of her to "have a hard time with praise." I encouraged her to talk with someone about this issue, because I feared it could interfere with a promising career. She followed through on my suggestion and often voluntarily shared with me during our consultations her journey in self-discovery.

She had been sexually assaulted during childhood. One of the more terrible effects of child abuse is that the abused child often incorporates the identity given to him or her by the predator (Sabbath, 1969). One of those messages given by the experience of child abuse is: "You are worthless." This sense of worthlessness became ingrained in her personality and became one of her more personal demons. This sense of self often dictated how she thought, felt, and behaved. She could have chosen a defense method of prominently displayed self-importance and grandiosity to protect herself from these self-loathing assaults. Instead, she chose another defense mechanism. She engaged in cannabis use. In cannabis she found transient, temporary relief from her demons. She began cannabis use at the age of 12. It worked quite effectively to protect her. She became psychologically and physiologically addicted to the drug. She also chose her profession, as many people are inclined to do, as a self-protector from a sense of worthlessness. This sense of self-hate, self-devaluation, and self-disregard was the locus of her personal pain. It also contributed to her experiencing chronic suicide ideation.

"Deep inside," she would share with me, "I have this sense of worthlessness—that people, the world, would better off without me." There was no amount of cognitively focused logic that could undo her torture. Years of therapy with a skilled clinician has allowed this woman to achieve a life worth living and become a gift to our profession.

Suicide is a complexity. To understand this is to accept the individual and the idiosyncratic nature of the suicide event. Yet, all too often our need is to simplify this complexity. We struggle with ambiguities, shades of gray, nuances. We often want to categorize and organize suicide so that we feel more comfortable in understanding this tragic human behavior. Edwin Shneidman (1985) cautioned us when he said of suicide: "Suicide is the result of an untimely convergence of multiple psychiatric, psychological, social, relational, environmental, occupational, cultural, medical, academic stressors that severely challenges an individual's capacity to cope."

We have just discussed the risk factors for suicide in people with co-occurring disorders. These conditions create in an individual a vulnerability to consider suicide as a management strategy for unbearable levels of pain (Jacobs & Brown, 1989; Moscicki, 1997). These conditions, when observed in our clients, should trigger further inquiry on the subject of suicide. These are the issues of early intervention.

SUICIDAL POPULATIONS

Let us, therefore, surrender to the human need to organize, categorize, and label suicide for a better understanding of this human tragedy. Suicide is best understood in terms of the individualized experience. No two people experience the tragedy of suicide in an identical fashion. Suicide is, as mentioned previously, an idiosyncratic experience. We would like to offer the reader, however, a categorization of the suicide experience with a discussion of how the wish to die is actualized. We will now present our conceptualization of this event and how it is presented in three different methods: suicide ideation, suicide attempts, and suicide completion.

The Suicide Ideator

David Clark, PhD, an epidemiologist with Rush Research Center in Chicago, noted years ago: "Dying from suicide is quite rare; thinking about suicide is very common." Research in several settings reveals that possibly hundreds of thousands of people contemplate ending their lives in any given year. Suicide ideation, or thinking about suicide, is a period of time (with the time span identified by the person) where levels of stress become so unbearable that they defy that person's capacity to cope. Suicide thoughts are entertained as coping strategies and problem solvers—a method of eliminating these personally defined levels of emotional, psychological, and psychiatric pain. It was mentioned early in this chapter that clients define their locus of pain. We accept and are empathic to their individual definition of where they hurt. The ideator sees death as the end of this pain, often looking forward to "nothingness" (Shneidman, 1985).

Let us explore this population and emphasize some markers that are important to understand:

- *Suicide ideation is a very common experience.* Because of this feature, we respect that all people are vulnerable to this experience. Suicide ideation has no respect for age, gender, race, culture, educational status, religious affiliation, or socioeconomic status. The profile of the ideator is all inclusive. The necessary stimulus for this event—the unbearable pain—can be experienced by anybody.

- *Suicide ideation is never pathologized.* For the ideator suicide is seen, at this moment in time, as a very reasonable and attractive problem-solving strategy. We are, in fact, empathic to the period of ideation. It is understandable. We offer you the example of a 58-year-old woman who suddenly loses her husband to a heart attack. He is walking out of church on a beautiful Sunday morning, collapses, and dies. He dies one month before his retirement—an event he and his wife had been eagerly anticipating. He is a wonderful husband, father, friend, and person. The woman is devastated by her grief. She begins to cope by drinking, which provides her with transient relief. She then begins to seek permanent relief with thoughts of death and suicide. Due to the intensity of the pain, these thoughts become yearnings. For this woman, at this period of her life, suicide is viewed as the only option out of her grief.

- *Suicide ideators are ambivalent about their suicidal thoughts.* This ambivalence stems from many factors. The most important is that the ideator still has hope. This hope is often fragile, unrealistic, and merely wishful thinking, but it is still hope. Hopelessness—fatalistic despair—is the most powerful fueling emotion to suicide. Suicide is the direct result of despair and hopelessness. If people have even a shred of hope that things in their life may improve and get better, that issue may keep them alive.

- *Suicide ideators openly communicate their suicidal fears.* They will eagerly discuss with you the locus of their pain. They will talk about their lack of coping and the wish to die. Ideators are open to counseling, are very motivated in counseling, and have an excellent prognosis.

- *Finally, we should hospitalize this group only with extreme caution.* A few markers that could encourage us to use inpatient services for temporary safety include (a) the ideator has very detailed plans on how he or she would die and has access to lethal means; (b) the ideator is currently using drugs to manage the unbearable pain; (c) the ideator has a sense of peace and calm when thoughts of death are entertained; and (d) the ideator sees no benefit to remaining alive and has no emotional/psychological barrier to keep him or her from death. More often than not, however, ideators are seen as very appropriate candidates for outpatient counseling. They never act on the suicide wish. Ideators do not make suicide attempts and they do not die from suicide.

The Suicide Attempter

This term is widely misunderstood and misused in mental health service delivery systems. Part of what we want to accomplish here is to clarify exactly what a suicide attempt is and what it is not. We also want to comment on some activities that are often confused with these acts. Suicide attempters are people who have an intent to die. Their goal is death. This intent distinguishes the attempt and the ideation. The critical issue here, however, is that a history of suicide attempts is a powerful correlate to eventual death by suicide. Any client with a history of suicide attempts should be taken very seriously and attended with caution. Let us examine this behavior and describe this population.

A suicide attempter is an individual who has committed a potentially lethal act where the intent was to die. The activity was, however, reversible (cutting, slashing, overdosing, gassing), and the attempter was accidentally rescued, against his or her wishes, with the result that he or she survived. As an example, a young man, who was severely depressed about his inability to overcome a serious drug dependency issue, decided to take his life. His mother left for work each morning at 6 a.m. and did not return until 4 p.m. One morning he gave his mother a half-hour to get to work, then ran a hot bath, cut both of his arms with a razor, and began to bleed.

His mother, on her way to work, realized she had forgotten the keys to her building and turned her car around to return home to get her keys. Because the young man's car was still in the driveway, she came into the house, called his name, and got no response. She walked up the stairs, saw her son bleeding in the bathtub, called the local emergency response number, and saved his life. That is a suicide attempt. The issue is that if the mother had not forgotten her work keys, this young man would have died. The circumstances of rescue lead us to the conclusion that his rescue was accidental and against his wishes. We must capture this intent in our clients, because this history is a powerful correlate to eventual death by suicide. It may also guide us to the focal point of the clients' pain and may, perhaps, provide us with a central focus of therapy.

A reversible suicide activity is an act where, from the beginning of the activity to the moment it leads to death, there is a brief window of time for rescue. Cutting, slashing, overdosing, and gassing are common reversible activities; from the moment a person takes a razor to the skin there is an opportunity for rescue before that act causes death. Sometimes that activity is accidentally interrupted and, at other times, it is self-interrupted. I remember hearing one of the rare survivors of a leap off the Golden Gate Bridge claim, "as soon as my hand left the rail, I knew I made a mistake." That is a sobering comment. Many of you may have seen data on attempters versus completers. If you have, you will have noticed that the majority of attempters are female, whereas the majority of completers are male. One reason for this divergence is that females more often use reversible methods, whereas males usually employ irreversible methods such as shooting or hanging—methods where there is no window for rescue.

Therefore, in another category of suicide attempts is the person who has committed a potentially lethal act where the intent is to die, but it is reversible, and in a panic they self-interrupt. In this panic state, after they seek rescue, they often need immediate medical attention or they will die. That is a suicide attempt. The key issue in this population is a state of panic. They often beg, during rescue, "Don't let me die." An example is a young woman, who was recently rejected in an intimate relationship. She impulsively takes a razor to her arms and begins to bleed. She panics, calls for rescue, and is taken to a local emergency room, where she needs immediate medical attention or she will die from a loss of blood. She claims to the ER staff: "I wanted to die, but when I saw all the blood I went into a panic." This panic state has received quite a bit of attention from studies. It appears to be the result of a sudden, jolting awareness of impending death. It is ironic that when studying suicide one is confronted with so many incongruent features. One minute the person is yearning for death as a way out of unbearable pain and then, when confronted with the reality of death, there is that life-saving panic, a result of the survival instinct.

The final category of suicide attempters are people who have a degree of certainty, often wrongly assessed, that a specific activity will terminate their existence. The activity fails to achieve that goal, and they are significantly upset at this failure. They will often claim afterward: "I can't even kill myself the right way." An example would be an adolescent, recently rejected in a meaningful relationship, who responds by swallowing a handful of his parent's antidepressant medication and lying down waiting to die. Seven hours later he is still alive and very upset. Such attempters will often tell the parent what they did. The key is for that brief moment they had an intent to die, and they are very angry that they did not succeed. Depending on how this act is addressed by the individual or the social support system, this person may continue to entertain thoughts of suicide and revisit a life-threatening activity at a later date.

These three activities are usually seen as the common locus of describing suicide attempts, but we must differentiate them from other behaviors that are often mistakenly termed as attempts. These behaviors range from nonlethal self-mutilation behaviors to suicide gesturing to calculated self-harm activities for secondary gain. An examination of these behaviors is important because it helps us describe with clarity behaviors that are truly suicide attempts.

Nonsuicidal self-injurious behavior, or self-mutilation, is differentiated from suicide attempts by the issue of intent. The intent of suicide is to eliminate and terminate unbearable pain. The intent of self-mutilation is to continue to live and to manage pain. In fact, self-mutilation is often seen as a protector from completed suicide. In many circumstances self-mutilation can be seen as a behavior that actually keeps a person from thinking about or attempting suicide. In no way is this designed to reduce our concern over the issue of self-mutilation. We remain alert to this behavior; however, we are cautious in labeling this population as suicidal. Again, the issue of intent is of utmost importance. A young woman who cuts her wrists in order to manage her vulnerability to disassociation can hardly be called suicidal because her intent for the act of cutting is distinctly different from a young man who slashes his wrists in order to bleed to death. The treatments for both populations do have similarities, but the caution of using inpatient programs with the suicide attempter is going to be much more important than seeking a similar setting for the nonsuicidal self-mutilator.

At a conference I attended many years ago, Alan Berman discussed the concept of behavioral reversal for suicide. He talked about his familiarity with people who died by suicide and, prior to their death, practiced the activity that was eventually used to take their lives. He remarked on the individual who died by hanging and, prior to his death, was found tying a rope or tightening a belt around his neck. He assumed that this person, and many like him, were rehearsing the suicide act. The goal, he assumed, was to become familiar with the activity, to get used to it for the purpose of decreasing the anxiety connected with ending one's life. These people are commonly referred to as suicide gestures. They are planning suicide with the activities and should be taken very seriously. They are not, however, suicide attempters. At the time of their activity they are not intending to die; the goal is to practice the activity to decrease the associated anxiety. It is important to understand the hierarchy from the self-mutilator who is cutting in a calculated fashion in order to get relief from anxiety to the suicide gesture who is cutting to get familiar with how the razor feels against skin, as opposed to the person who is cutting for the purposes of exsanguination and eventual death—the suicide attempter/completer.

Finally, it is important to discuss people who use suicidal threats and/or calculated self-harm activities for secondary gain. As we revisit our consideration of goals that motivate behaviors, we discover in these people some fascinating dynamics. It has been well documented in the works of Linehan (1993) that people with features of borderline personality disorder have significant difficulty in dealing with stress, regulating emotions, and tolerating rejection and abandonment in relationships. These conditions may motivate

140

them to use threats of suicide or calculated self-harm activities to gain access to settings that may help them achieve management over these challenging events and resultant emotions. These people are not acutely suicidal, but they present as such to gain help with their issues. These presentations come in different shapes and sizes. They are, however, recognized by the goal of secondary gain. Examples are numerous: "If you don't put me in the hospital, I'm going to kill myself"; "If you leave me, I'm going to kill myself"; "If you fire me, I'm going to kill myself." They present with varied levels of risk: The homeless individual who presents in a hospital's emergency room threatening suicide on a subfreezing night to gain access to shelter for the night; or the individual recently charged with a crime who uses suicide threats to gain access to a psychiatric facility for the purpose of assisting in his legal defense; or the young man who threatens to kill himself if his current girlfriend leaves him as she has just threatened to do; or the young woman severely lacking in emotional regulation skills and stress tolerance skills who, in a frenzied state, seeks hospitalization to soothe her emotional discomfort. We treat all of these people with respect and dignity and, as we will discuss, we do treat them.

As we conclude our discussion on suicide attempts, we need to emphasize the vital importance of capturing in your client a history that is positive for this behavior. On average, over their lifetimes, about 10% to 15% of individuals with a history of clearly defined suicide attempts eventually go on to take their lives (Roy & Linnoila, 1990). A history that is positive for clearly defined suicide attempts is considered a primary risk factor and correlate to eventual death by suicide. It is, therefore, strongly recommended that all agencies and clinicians routinely screen new clients or patients for history of suicide activity.

The Suicide Completer

The term *suicide completer* is used to describe people who died by suicide. They pursue an activity that they know, if allowed to go unattended, will kill them. Death is the ultimate intent of this activity. These types of activities are fueled by two vital emotions for suicide: hopelessness and helplessness. Ronald Maris (1992) spoke of this hopelessness when he discussed the process of suicide. He states:

> One key to predicting suicide is that lifelong repetition of similar problems reaching an interactive threshold in some individuals, but not in others. We need to know why this happens. Apparently, almost anyone can and routinely does survive single, acute crises. Hopelessness leading to suicide is an emotion made up of very different stuff—repeated loss, repeated depression, repeated hospitalizations, chronic aloneness, chronic physical pain, chronic emotional pain, progressive loss of social support, repeated failures, and any other condition that wears the person out.

This issue of hopelessness is the primary feature in the identification of the high-risk suicide completer. The helplessness of completers is evidenced by weakened self-validation: They do not see themselves as capable of solving life's problems. This penetrating awareness of being inept creates the lethal elements of self-directed rage and devaluation. The profile of the suicide completer contains elements that all clinicians must be aware of.

Markers for the suicide completer are as follows: male, white, and 25 years of age or older; being separated, widowed, or divorced; living alone and/or having no sense of social cohesion; being unemployed or retired; being in poor physical health; having a medical mental disorder of mood, anxiety, and/or psychosis; drug dependency (predominantly alcohol dependency); having visited a primary care physician within six months of the suicide death; having a history positive for suicide attempts where firearms, hanging, or jumping was the method and the individual was immediately rescued by accidental discovery and against his wishes; not reporting suicide intent to others and/or no suicide intent communication; and leaving a suicide note. An actual suicide is particularly likely when there is significant social isolation, when there are significant elements of a mental disorder, and when substance use is designed to manage and/or control the symptoms of a mental disorder (co-occurring disorders or the self-medicating mentally ill). Verbalizing metaphors of hopelessness and helplessness are also seen as significant correlates to completed suicide. The most concerning element in this profile is a lack of indication about suicide intent (Maris, 1992). Allow me to operationalize some of these elements with a case showing how these issues may be displayed by clients.

A 44-year-old white male was ordered into treatment by the local drug court diversion program. The initial mental status exam conducted during intake revealed some diagnostic and treatment concerns. He appeared for his intake session in a timely fashion. Dress and grooming were of concern, as he was wearing a thin coat when temperatures were below freezing. His clothes were ragged and torn. Personal hygiene was of concern, as he had a distinct body odor and was poorly groomed. His attitude was passive, with an economy of speech and responses. He established poor eye contact, and his affect was subdued with a dysphoric mood. He appeared much older than his stated age and had a continuous, productive cough. His fingers were nicotine stained, and he asked repeatedly if he could smoke during our session. He was visibly agitated and upset when I denied him that request. He indicated that his sleep, appetite, and energy levels were poor. He was currently homeless and indicated that, with few exceptions, this has been his state for more than 20 years. His only source of pleasure was "smoking crack." He indicated that he started using cocaine while he was in college, and he had been using continuously for more than 20 years. He was oriented to time, place, person, and reason for interview. He did not display any bizarre or delusional thoughts. When he did engage in conversation, he showed a high level of intelligence. He left college after his second year of courses in prelaw, and he refused to elaborate on the circumstances of his terminating his education.

He made it very clear during the interview that he was not with me of his own volition. He was coerced by the court. His use of projection, blame, denial of personal responsibility, and rationalizing behaviors were pronounced defense mechanisms. He indicated that he had no intention of stopping his drug use and said: "Telling me to quit my cocaine is like telling me to stop breathing." He was reluctant to discuss childhood issues other than to say he was "estranged from my parents at a very early age." When asked to elaborate, he refused by telling me: "That's none of your business." He stated that he was married and divorced twice and has four children, two from each marriage. He again refused to provide further information on family or marital issues. He did, however, add that he had not "seen my kids in years, I have no idea where they are." There was a hint of sadness in this reply, and when I reflected that, he became very defensive and wanted to know "what this has to do with my drug use." I asked him about friends, and he laughed and said "my crack buddies." He then spontaneously offered: "I don't even know their names, we just get high together." He then offered: "Nobody out there gives me a thought."

I asked about medical care, and he reported that he hadn't been seen by a medical professional in more than 20 years. When asked about employment history, he indicated that he has an "aimless existence." He did refer to a history of periodic part-time employment in janitorial, maintenance, and dishwashing jobs. They usually lasted three or four weeks. Then he would quit. He stated: "I get bored easily." I asked about other drug use, and he indicated that while cocaine is predominant, he also drinks. He voluntarily added: "When I am lonely I'll go to a bar and have a few beers just to have somebody to talk to. You know, people like me better when I'm drunk. When I'm drunk I can be an entertaining guy." When asked what crack cocaine does for him, he said, "it keeps me alert and helps me stay awake."

He acknowledged nighttime traumas. He said he served in the military and was in Vietnam for a year. When I asked for further information on his military experience, he shut me down: "That is one thing I do not want to talk about and you need to get that very clear right now." He denied any history of treatment for substance use or mental health concerns. When I asked about a history of suicide activity, he mentioned an attempt when he was younger. He elaborated by adding: "I tried to hang myself, but someone found me." He refused to talk about the circumstances of rescue, but added: "I think about it every day." I asked him if he were to decide upon suicide as a solution, whether he would share his plans with another person. His response was: "Who would I tell? Nobody gives a damn about me. Even if somebody did care, I probably wouldn't say anything."

Edwin Shneidman made a comment years ago that was quite chilling. In a chapter of his very last book, he began: "In this chapter I want to tell you about a man I met once who I knew was eventually going to die by suicide and there was nothing I could do about it" (Shneidman, 1993). I had a similar sense with this man, but we never give up or lose hope with our clients. I believe that Shneidman was trying to tell us that we do the best we can, but there are times where we may not succeed in keeping our clients alive. This man certainly met the criteria for high risk for completed suicide. What was fascinating about him was that in his initial session he gave me a gift—he articulated his locus of pain. He told me where he hurt, and I jumped on it. Clinicians never turn down a gift. He told me where he hurt, and if he was going to engage in therapy at all, this was the topic he would consider discussing. He gave me a small opening, a brief invitation, and I accepted.

WHO IS AT RISK?

When are we supposed to know a person is at risk for suicide? What, exactly, are we assessing? We have been told over the years that the prediction of suicide is extremely difficult, if not impossible. Motto urged us to respect the use of and limitations of suicide assessments and prediction scales. He said:

> Suicide prediction scales are explicit psychological test instruments that are designed to standardize information transfer from the potentially suicidal person to the clinician. Because of the low frequency of suicide and the dire consequences of an error in the judgment that a person is not suicidal, the development and evaluation of subscales are not to be seen as standard psychometric exercises. Indeed, even the possibility of prediction of this form of violent behavior continues to be debated. However our approach is that of focusing on the prediction of risk of the behavior rather than prediction of the behavior itself. That, we feel, would justify the continuing use and interest in the area of standardized suicide prediction scales. The evaluations, assessments, and prediction scales will focus on information that the clinician needs to make decisions about the probable future actions of the distressed patient. (Motto, 1985)

Ronald Maris made an even more cautionary statement when he said: "One might cynically conclude that the only suicide predictor is the suicide itself" (Maris, 1992).

We talked earlier about the complicated and dangerous profile of the suicide completer. They are defined in various ways. There are, however, commonalities among them. They have a cognitive awareness that the activity they are ready to engage in creates a significant risk of ending in their death. Indeed, their goal is death. This is the essential component of the definition of suicide. An act cannot be termed a suicide unless there was, on the part of the deceased, a clearly established intent to die. Finally, suicide completers typically engage in highly lethal means to ensure that outcome. From data gathered by psychological autopsies and death certificates, it is known that the profile of the suicide completer is usually as follows: They are male and Caucasian; living alone; have a loss of occupational definition, experiencing a mood, anxiety, or psychotic disorder; are self-medicating with drugs and/or alcohol; not in therapy at the time of their death; no direct suicide communication; and experiencing issues of fatalism, despair, and severe self-devaluation.

In my own practice I have had many experiences with the dynamics of this profile, especially the dynamic of "no intent communication." Many years ago, my practice conducted a Survivors of Suicide support group. This group met every other week for people who had lost a loved one to suicide. One evening a grieving pair of parents, who had lost their 28-year-old son to suicide, brought in a tape their son had made right before his death. They wanted me to review the tape to determine if it would be appropriate to play for the group members at our next meeting. I did review the tape and felt it would be very appropriate for this group to hear their son's last comments before his death.

The tape started with their son saying goodbye to the family. His voice was subdued, quiet, and he sounded quite sad and depressed. But his words were soothing, loving, and calm—designed to alleviate any sense of guilt or responsibility that the family might have had as a result of his choice. In the middle of the tape, the phone rang. He left his taping for a few minutes to answer the phone, but he left the recorder on, and it captured his phone conversation. It was his grandmother who was calling. In his conversation with his grand-mother, he appeared to be enthusiastic, happy, verbal, and engaging. He talked to his grandmother about his wish to buy a new car, looking for a new job, and many other issues that were going on in his life. Finally, he mentioned to his grandmother that he had to be going and said to her as he concluded the conversation, "Remember, grandma, I love you, and I will see you on Sunday for dinner." After the phone call was concluded, he went back to the tape and, for one final moment, said a tearful goodbye to his family—and then you heard the gunshot. No more than 30 seconds before this young man terminated his existence he had said to his grandmother, "I love you, and I will see you on Sunday for dinner."

It may appear, from this information, that identifying the suicide completer in advance is a difficult, if not almost impossible, task. It is a challenge, but we need to be aware of certain behaviors in our efforts to recognize and capture the suicide completer population. First, usu-ally within six weeks of a suicide act, suicide completers experience significant psychological and/or psychiatric turmoil. Their eating hab-its change, sleeping habits change, and they are more irritable than usual. They may have significant difficulty in concentration, and their symptoms of depression, anxiety, and/or psychosis become greatly enhanced. They often verbalize hopelessness and helplessness. The reader is encouraged to remain alert to metaphors of fatalistic despair and significant self-devaluation, which are the two primary ingredi-ents to the emotions of hopelessness and helplessness.

It is also known that prior to the suicide act that completers present with anhedonia and dysphoria. Anhedonia is a demonstrated inability to gain pleasure from behaviors that, at one time, had given the person pleasure. Dysphoria is literally an emotional shutdown. Shneidman told us many years ago that "people who die by suicide die emotionally before they die physically." Suicide completers, prior to their death, demonstrate a morbid preoccupation with the past. This is often their recounting of a life full of regrets, and it is the only thing they can talk about. They will discuss regrets over choosing the wrong profession, not saving enough money, not being a good parent, or not being a good enough spouse or partner. They also, on occasion, provide us with remote suicide communication, which is often metaphoric. It is phrased as a current apathy toward life and an anticipation toward death. Suicide completers demonstrate a refusal to seek help when encouraged to do so by friends or family members. When these behaviors are observed, it is essential that a safety setting—ideally, a psychiatric inpatient facility—be pursued.

However, the most significant and lethal of all of these markers is the rapid change from turmoil to peacefulness and tranquility. It has been referred to, in various readings, as the "amazing reversal." It is a very rapid change from the turmoil spoken of previously to a state of tranquility, calmness, and peacefulness. During this time clients deny any suicide intent and do not display any of the behaviors of concern. For the therapist, this dynamic could become your worst nightmare. Let me give you an example.

A few years ago I received a phone call from the mother of a man in his mid-thirties. She was calling me out of concern for her son, whom she said had just been released from a psychiatric inpatient unit. Apparently, he was released because his insurance benefits expired. She was concerned that his discharge was premature, and she was very concerned that he was still at risk. According to the mother, the family had hospitalized her son because he was severely depressed after the breakup of a long-term relationship. The reason for her call was to find out if he still needed to be hospitalized. I spoke to her for a while about different options, and then she asked me if I would be willing to see her son to determine if he still needed inpatient care. I told her to have him give me a call.

About one hour later, this man called me, and we arranged for an appointment later that afternoon. The man showed up for his appointment in a timely fashion, dressed appropriately for the weather. His mental status exam was uncomplicated. He was oriented to time, place, person, and reason for interview. His thoughts were logically and coherently presented, and eye contact was excellent. His affect and mood were congruent with circumstances. He had excellent futuristic thinking and, overall, the one hour and 45-minute interview appeared, on the surface, to be nonproblematic. During the entire interview, he denied any current suicide ideation or intent and proclaimed significant optimism about his relationship with his girlfriend. As I have gone over this case many times in my mind over the years, the one issue that for me significantly stands out was the fact that he presented as being "almost too good." I did have a sense of unease about his presentation, and I commented in the mental status exam about my concern around the validity of his presentation.

During this conversation, I made several attempts to engage him in conversation aimed at a discovery of pain. He refused these attempts and instead continued his avoidance of any material that could be seen as problematic or concerning. Toward the end of the conversation, I offered continued counseling, and he refused. He responded to these offers by thanking me for my concern and emphasizing that he was "feeling much better," had no suicide intent, and did not need therapy at this time in his life.

At the end of our time together, I gave him my card and encouraged him to call with any concerns. Approximately five hours later, I received a phone call from the man's mother informing me that she had just been notified of her son's death. A police officer had just visited her with the news about finding her son behind his garage that evening. He was dead from a self-inflicted gunshot to the head. He died no more than an hour or two from the time he left my office.

This man represents a classic example of the amazing reversal. As I mentioned, it could present the clinician with a significant challenge. In most states, in order to place someone in a psychiatric facility against his will, a very specific process must be pursued. That process includes a recognition that the person is demonstrating behaviors associated with a mental disorder. Furthermore, because of those mental disorders, the person must be seen as dangerous to self, dangerous to others, or unable to care for personal needs. If the clinician observes such behaviors, he or she is mandated to begin the process of involuntary hospitalization. During my interview of over one hour with this man, he, unfortunately, gave me no information that could fit that criterion. The message here is quite clear: The earlier we capture the suicide completer, the more enhanced our outcome might be. If we delay our interventions to a point where the amazing reversal becomes a reality, the outcome may be tragic.

As we conclude this chapter, I would like to summarize some of the more important features we have discussed. In all assessments, whether it be for the ideator, the attempter, or the completer, it is essential to remember to assess people and not behaviors. It is encouraged, therefore, that when standardized tests and measurements are used for assessment purposes, they only be used to validate or invalidate our clinical judgment. We should never rely on a standardized test or measurement as a stand-alone assessment for suicide. Assessments are not designed to predict suicide. Assessments are designed, primarily, to gain insight into risk factors that clients may present that would make them vulnerable to self-harm behaviors. It is extremely important for clinicians to remember that society does not expect us to predict the future. What society does expect of us is to assess risk factors for specific behaviors.

Hindsight into suicide is always 20/20. We must continuously keep in mind that the act of suicide for our clients is a unique experience to them. Our clients travel down the road to the tragedy of suicide on their own individual paths. Our task is to do the best we possibly can to understand people's struggles in life. It is important that we always do the best we can, because it is what society expects of us and what we should expect of ourselves.

CHAPTER SEVEN

Putting It All Together — Integrated Treatment

Chapter 1 discussed the essential aspect of guiding people with co-occurring disorders by the strategy of integrated treatment (Minkoff, 2004). In this strategy, Minkoff is proposing to us the need for therapy flexibility. This capacity, in the primary treatment relationship, encourages us to integrate appropriate diagnosis-specific interventions for each disorder into a client-centered cohesive treatment plan. This plan is constantly being evaluated with the flexibility to modify each diagnostic approach as the treatment relationship unfolds. The one consistent in all of this will be the constant, caring relationship.

This being said, it would be easy to dismiss this chapter, and reduce its impact, into a mere statement of "you're on your own." Although we do know many evidence-based therapy approaches for the specific disorders that we are going to encounter, the key to successful treatment is always going to be this flexibility, which will allow us to adroitly maneuver our approach to meet the changing nuances of people with co-occurring disorders. This flexibility will be displayed in the foundation of the ongoing, caring, constant relationship.

However, throughout all of this maneuvering will be the ongoing influence of several guiding principles. Whichever treatment approach the clinician decides to utilize will be influenced by these essential guiding principles. In this chapter, therefore, we will not address the multiple evidence-based therapies that have been proven to be efficacious for people with co-occurring disorders. Instead, this chapter examines the guiding principles of the therapy relationship and approach. These guiding principles incorporate the clients' view in a holistic fashion. Although a diagnosis-specific perception of clients is necessary, that diagnosis can never be the singular determinant of treatment. It is essential that we get to know our clients. They will be matched to treatment services based on a variety of clinical factors and levels of functioning in their world. They will not be placed under an arranged treatment program based only on having met specific diagnostic criteria. Our clients are remarkably complex. Our treatment plan for them, therefore, must respect that complexity.

Donald Meichenbaum once said, "All therapy approaches have holes!" (Meichenbaum, 2010). He is so very correct. Evidence-based therapies are not, as I am sure many of you are aware, guaranteed to bring our clients to health. Many evidence-based therapies work for some of clients and not for others. I believe that Dr. Meichenbaum was trying to impress upon us that all treatment approaches have limitations. Also, I am relatively sure that many of the readers of this book are already acquainted with the intricacies of cognitive-behavioral therapy, dialectical behavioral therapy, exposure therapy for PTSD, and many of the other fascinating approaches we have that work to alleviate the pain of the human condition. Therefore, this chapter focuses on the intricacies of the guiding principles for treatment and does not belabor the well-known tenets of the more popular and efficacious treatment approaches.

Case conceptualization was previously defined in Chapter 5. It was stressed that the case conceptualization of clients is the absolute, essential first step in the formulation of an effective treatment plan. Case conceptualization, however, should also include a respect for who we, the clinicians, are. Consider the following questions: What do we, as individuals, bring to the therapy process? What are our strengths and weaknesses? What personal issues allow us to work effectively with this diverse population? And what personal issues

152

may challenge us in effectively working with certain populations in our society? Finally, who exactly are we as clinicians? In what type of therapy environment do we toil? What are our boundaries? What is the mission statement of our practice or the agency in which we serve our population? In other words, our first task is to have a case conceptualization of who we are in the professional realm.

David Mee-Lee and Ken Minkoff offer us some suggestions for this self-definition. These categories are essential to respect. We all need to be aware of who we are individually, as a practice, or as an agency. In this self-definition process, we are going to define our program capabilities. This professional self-exploration allows us the guidance to determine who among the co-occurring disorder population we can see and who we should refer to other practitioners or agencies.

The ASAM PPC-2R (Patient Placement Criteria — Second Revision) defines program capabilities as being of three types:

1. *Programs that offer addiction-only services.* These programs cannot accommodate patients with psychiatric illnesses who require ongoing treatment, however stable the illness and however well-functioning the individual. Such programs are said to provide addiction-only services. The policies and procedures typically do not accommodate co-occurring disorders. For example, individuals on psychotropic medications generally are not accepted, coordination or collaboration with medical services is not routinely present, and mental health issues are not usually addressed in treatment planning for content.

2. *Dual-diagnosis-capable programs.* These programs routinely accept individuals who have co-occurring mental and substance-related disorders. Dual-diagnosis-capable programs can meet such patients' needs so long as their psychiatric disorders are sufficiently stabilized and the individuals are capable of independent functioning to such a degree that their mental disorders do not interfere with participation in addiction treatment. Dual-diagnosis-capable programs address dual diagnoses in the policies and procedures, assessments, treatment planning, program

content, and discharge planning. These programs have arrangements in place for coordination and collaboration with mental health services. These programs can also provide psychopharmacologic monitoring and psychological assessment and consultation on site or by a well-coordinated consultation on site.

3. *Dual-diagnosis-enhanced programs.* These programs can accommodate individuals with dual diagnoses who may be unstable or disabled to such an extent that specific psychiatric and mental health support monitoring and accommodation are essential in order for them to participate in addiction treatment. Such patients are not as acute or impaired as to present a severe danger to self or others, nor do they require 24-hour psychiatric supervision. Dual-diagnosis-enhanced programs are staffed by psychiatric and mental health clinicians as well as addiction professionals. Cross training is provided to all staff. Such programs tend to have relatively high staff-to-patient ratios and provide close monitoring of patients who demonstrate psychiatric instability and disability. These programs typically have policies, procedures, assessments, treatment planning and discharge planning, and accommodate patients with dual diagnoses. Dual-diagnosis-specific and mental health symptom management groups are incorporated into addiction treatment. Motivational enhancement therapies are more likely to be available, particularly if this program is in an outpatient setting. Ideally, there is close collaboration or integration with a mental health program that provides crisis backup services and access to mental health case management and continuing care.

With this understanding, let us present a case example and, perhaps, a dilemma. The pastor of a local church refers to your private practice a man for whom he has significant worry and concern. He describes this individual in the following fashion: The referral is in his "late sixties or early seventies," has been homeless for years, is reportedly in and out of jail for charges of vagrancy and public drunkenness, and is reportedly often seen talking to himself. The pastor knows that this man is an alcohol user, and he also suspects that he uses multiple drugs. It appears that the individual has a legal guardian who manages the money he receives from the Veterans Administration. The person is, according to stories the pastor has heard, a decorated Vietnam War combat veteran. Over the years the pastor has known this individual, he has consistently refused services. The pastor feels, however, that his "attitude might be changing" because, during a recent conversation with the person, he made the comment, "I cannot continue to live like this."

You practice alone, and based on the above definitions you would best describe your practice as addiction-only services. After considerable thought and consideration, there is a very real probability that you are going to decline the pastor's request and suggest a more comprehensive program for this person. Your decision on this issue came from the honest conceptualization of you and your individual private practice. Basically, you are not professionally equipped to serve this man in the fashion in which he deserves. In other words, you have a clear understanding of what you are capable of doing and those situations in which your engagement would be ill advised.

The reader may recall our quote from Donald Meichenbaum when he said: "Therapy without case conceptualization is like a boat without a rudder, wandering aimlessly through the water with no sense of direction." It is, therefore, essential to have an overall perspective, or case conceptualization, of not only ourselves and the entity in which we work but also our clients. Many people with co-occurring disorders have a relatively low severity level of substance use and low impairment from the effects of mental disorders. These people, for example, may experience periods of dysthymia or chronic depression that does not interfere with their social, relational, occupational, or vocational endeavors. They may, however, discover when they use alcohol they experience a transient, temporary, but wonderful, release from that depression. They experience an internal sense of well-being, enhanced capacity for social interaction, and an overall elevation in their engagement with life. They may begin to experience, however, after a certain period of time, a sense of being addicted to the alcohol. They will come running to your office or agency.

They are quite dismayed and worried, because this relatively new discovery of being addicted has presented to them an uncomfortable reaction in their social, relational, and occupational endeavors. Because of the dystonic reaction to this condition, and because it powerfully interferes with issues they value in their lives, these people are powerfully motivated in therapy and have an excellent prognosis. They will be seen on an outpatient basis only. Medication indicated for the possible psychiatric disorder of depression will be initiated. Individual counseling efforts aimed at resolving the dystonic condition will be initiated. Support groups for the addiction issues may be initiated during this outpatient involvement.

Another example in this format of case conceptualization would be a man in his mid-forties who has experienced a lifelong condition of untreated, undetected generalized anxiety disorder. He discovered, many years ago, that when he engaged in cannabis use he achieved a transient, but very effective, ability to feel relaxation without worry. After a significant period of time he also began to experience a very powerful yearning and fondness for the drug, significant physical symptoms when there is an extended period of time without the drug, increasingly desperate actions to acquire the drug, and the symptoms of the drug use resulting in significant impairment in social, relational, and occupational functioning. This man is totally confused and dismayed because he had the misperception that he was engaging with a very benign drug. He had the misperception that he was smoking his "grandfather's marijuana." He literally had no idea that today's cannabis is significantly addictive.

Because of increased symptoms of physiologic addiction, and because the symptoms significantly interfere with important areas of functioning, he (and others like him) comes running to your agency or office. These people are also powerfully motivated in therapy because their drug use has become a very dystonic behavior. These people will also be seen on an outpatient basis only, and medication indicated for the possible psychiatric disorder of generalized anxiety will be initiated. Support groups for the addiction issues may be initiated during this outpatient involvement. These people will engage in individual counseling efforts aimed at resolving their dystonic reaction. They have an excellent prognosis.

We may also encounter a case that incorporates the dynamics of the following: A man in his mid-forties who has a longstanding diagnosis of schizophrenia spectrum disorder with a co-occurring diagnosis of alcohol use disorder with physiological dependence. He is currently under the case management services of the local community mental health organization. He is living in a group home and attending a day treatment program. He has frequent episodes of intoxication, which often make the active phase symptoms of his schizophrenia more pronounced. Although his symptom display in the realm of his schizophrenia is not seen as dangerous to self or others, it is disruptive to the ongoing routine of the group home.

In his history he has had multiple inpatient episodes or exacerbations of his psychotic symptomology, multiple medically supervised detox episodes, and alcohol treatment episodes. When he has maintained his sobriety, it was only for brief periods. He has no support in the community other than the people who run the group home and his case manager. He displays very little motivation to change, because his perspective on his drinking is that "it doesn't hurt anybody." He does have a history of noncompliance with his medication, and during these periods he drinks more often and is usually hospitalized.

This case obviously incorporates more intense services and the need for more comprehensive services than an individual private practitioner would provide. This individual does qualify for continuing case management with an individual clinician, case management team, or an ACT program, depending on the intensity of the need. A dual-diagnosis-enhanced program may be indicated because of the severity of his needs. This man is also going to need unconditional support, access to crisis intervention, social support, psychosocial rehabilitation in a day treatment program, and housing support that will be respectful of his disability. The program that he is in will also administer and supervise his continued use of nonaddictive medication for his psychotic mental disorder. This nonaddictive medication will be continuous regardless of his substance use patterns.

His motivation to change will be monitored periodically to assess the style of intervention that will be utilized. He will be encouraged, for instance, to participate in abstinence-oriented addiction recovery programs, but this will not be mandated as a condition of treatment until the client is in an appropriate stage of motivation. When this man experiences decompensation during his mental illness episodes, he will, hopefully, have access to either a dual-diagnosis-capable or dual-diagnosis-enhanced inpatient psychiatric unit. During those times when he needs stabilization for his substance use issues, he will, hopefully, have access to a dual-diagnosis-capable or dual-diagnosis-enhanced detoxification program. In short, the active treatment plan that he receives is going to be much more specific, intense, and comprehensive than the treatment plan for someone who uses cannabis for transient relief from symptoms of generalized anxiety and whose current functioning is viewed as minimally impaired in the social, relational, vocational, and occupational realms.

Ken Minkoff has offered us a wonderfully crafted structure for matching treatment strategies for patients with specific types of mental disorders and/or personality disorders and substance use disorders with, or without, physiologic dependency. This follows his caution and advice that there is no individual, correct treatment approach to co-occurring disorders. He consistently reminds us that effective treatment for this population is "specific to their mental disorder diagnosis, substance use disorder diagnosis, and the stage of motivation observed in the client" (Minkoff, 1999). In this format, Dr. Minkoff guides us to a discovery of the four quadrants of co-occurring disorders and leads us to appropriate treatment structures that respond to the individual nature of each quadrant. This issue was discussed earlier as in Chapter 5 on case conceptualization.

For example, Dr. Minkoff talks to us about a population he would define as being in the Quadrant III category. They are defined as people with low levels of severity in their mental disorder (dysthymia) but significant severity in the realm of their addiction disorder (crack/cocaine and alcohol use disorders with physiologic dependency). He then thoroughly outlines the appropriate treatment plan, approach, and structure for this individual population. This individualized approach differs in its structure from individuals defined by other quadrants (Minkoff, 2001).

There are so many nuances to the effective treatment of people with co-occurring disorders that we may be tempted to run. It is a complexity, but so is life, and these people display the idiosyncratic features that most of our clients present during the course of treatment. If there ever was a population that represented the need for person-centered and individualized treatment planning, it is people with co-occurring disorders.

This presentation was my attempt and effort to offer to the reader the first of the guiding principles for the treatment of co-occurring disorders, which is discussed in the following section.

RESPECT THEIR COMPLEXITY

The New Hampshire-Dartmouth Integrated Dual Disorder Treatment (IDDT) model is an evidence-based practice that improves the quality of life for persons with co-occurring disorders by integrating substance abuse services with mental health services. The IDDT model utilizes biopsychosocial treatments (which combine pharmacological, psychological, educational, and social interventions) to address the needs of clients. The IDDT model promotes ongoing recovery from co-occurring substance abuse and mental disorders by providing service agencies with specific strategies for organizing and delivering services. It is a very complex and comprehensive model with many details pertaining to the client's individual nature.

With this comprehensive detail, however, results are achieved. "Research has shown that the IDDT model helps consumers achieve the best outcomes when the service agencies maintain fidelity to the principles of the model" (The New Hampshire-Dartmouth Integrated Dual Disorder Treatment Model, 2002). Therefore, the first guiding principle for effective treatment of co-occurring disorders is to not only respect the complexity of clients, but also to respect the need for comprehensive, complex, diagnosis-specific, motivation-specific, individually formulated treatment plans. I would like to explore a few of the features of the IDDT model and operationalize them from the perspective of a private practice.

I have had the privilege of working with a fascinating group of people over the years—people who are mandated into treatment. This population brings to your office a special menu of tasks: They often lack motivation; they enter therapy with a confrontational, resistant attitude; they mimic compliance merely to comply with their mandate and rid you from their lives; they argue and debate with you; and, at times, they are so resigned to their fate that they wish they were dead. I am sure that you would all agree that they are an interesting group. In the area of the country in which I practice, this population has a terrible time being authorized and seen for treatment. If they show up at an intake center under mandate—"my parole agent told me to get treatment"—they will not be authorized for treatment under state-funded programs. This practice is based on the belief that our precious resources should only be spent on those who are eager and motivated to get out from under the burden of substance use disorders. People who are not motivated, so the belief goes, waste our time and resources. This incredible, misguided theory is in total ignorance of a basic tenet of treatment for people with co-occurring disorders, which is that people mandated into treatment have the same outcomes of treatment that are achieved by those who seek treatment voluntarily (Meichenbaum, 2010). Isn't that interesting? Resistance is a stage of change (Prochaska, DiClemente, & Norcross, 1992). We can actually experience some success with these people by using the skills offered to us by William Miller and Stephen Rollnick in *Motivational Interviewing* (2002). In my practice, we welcome them through our doors.

But this process of motivation to change may take some time, and the question is: What should be done with this population of resistant clients before they discover their motivation to change? We may move toward harm-reduction strategies, which are the best we can accomplish at certain times in counseling. Harm-reduction strategies are operationalized at times where moving clients to sobriety/abstinence is either untimely or not possible because of their resistance. These skills hope to reduce the damage done to clients by their use of substances. Certainly, the readers of this book are aware that we have been practicing these harm-reduction strategies for decades.

Methadone clinics, driver's education programs, and many psycho-educational programs on drug/alcohol use are designed to reduce the occupational, social, relational, and vocational harm done by substance users. To operationalize harm-reduction strategies, we must follow a few guidelines: (1) always be where the client is; (2) remain patient; (3) refrain from mandating abstinence; and (4) continue to provide hope.

Recovery from co-occurring disorders is best accomplished in stages and increments of success. The IDDT model reinforces a focus addressed earlier where we spoke on the stages of change as a vehicle to ensure that we were always in the right place at the right time with our clients. IDDT refers to this as stage-wise interventions. Research suggests that people with co-occurring disorders gain the most confidence in their ability to recover and lead a life worth living when they experience incremental, behaviorally measured successes that are in line with their motivation to change specific aspects of their lives. These incremental successes are often the result of implementing harm-reduction strategies. Let me give you an example.

Many years ago, I had the privilege of working with a man in his mid-forties who was a Vietnam War combat veteran, displayed significant issues of PTSD, was dependent on alcohol and cocaine, and displayed specific personality attributes related to the antisocial personality disorder. He was referred to my practice by his parole agent, and he was under a mandate to remain abstinent and sober. He violated that mandate on a daily basis. He proudly proclaimed to anybody who would listen that he had no intention to embark on the journey of sobriety or abstinence. He would often laugh, ridicule, and debate me and his parole agent with significant confrontations on the issue of his drug use. He would often proclaim that he had no intention to stop using drugs, and he would often defy the parole agent to "send him back to prison" because he really "didn't care where he lived." He was strongly entrenched in the precontemplation stage of change, and he was highly invested in his resistance.

At the time of my intervention with this man, he was living in an historical area of Grand Rapids, Michigan. This area was very close to the downtown section of that city and was being restored to its original beauty by a very active urban activity group. He lived in one of the older homes in this neighborhood, which was being reclaimed by young families with children. One of his favorite activities in the afternoon was to sit on the front porch of his apartment and ridicule and verbally harass the children who were getting off the school bus and heading home. He would do this in a drunken state and did not hide the fact that he was intoxicated by stacking up his beer cans next to him on the front steps. He became a nuisance in the neighborhood, and his landlord was informed. His landlord gave him a 30-day notice to cease and desist from this behavior or he would be ejected and, more than likely, become homeless. In my state, people on parole cannot be homeless and, therefore, this status would result in his being returned to prison.

As this client and I talked about the situation, he again proclaimed that he had no intention of stopping or cutting back on his alcohol consumption. We did, however, agree that he would no longer sit on the porch in the afternoon and harass the children on their way home from school. This was done to respond to the landlord's wishes, keep him in his home, and keep him out of prison. My fondest wish, however, was that this incident would possibly motivate him to embark on his journey to sobriety, but it didn't. So, instead, I went with him into a harm-reduction strategy, which was the best I could hope for at that time and was basically designed to reduce the damage that his drinking was doing to him.

The IDDT model recommends *time-unlimited services* and remaining patient. This feature could be a challenge, especially when resources are limited. Research suggests, however, that people with co-occurring disorders experience cycles of relapse and recovery throughout their lives. Research also suggests that people with co-occurring disorders achieve the highest quality of life when they have access to services throughout their entire process of recovery, which could be the rest of their lives (Minkoff, 1999). Therefore, this model recommends to service agencies to provide services to clients throughout their lifespan, even when their symptoms are mild and or infrequent. The model also suggests that service agencies refrain from discharging consumers from treatment if they stop taking their medication or continue using alcohol or other drugs. This feature is based on the research that strongly suggests that setbacks, slips, and relapses will occur naturally as a part of a lifelong cycle of relapse and recovery (Minkoff, 1999).

This model is deeply invested in the frame of treatment referred to as *abstinence oriented*. It strongly suggests, as mentioned previously, that we refrain from abstinence-mandated treatment. This rather controversial framework is the result of ample research suggesting that abstinence-mandated therapy is not effective. One reason often cited for this finding is in the nature of abstinence-mandated approaches. One of our hopes for our clients is that they become invested in their program. I am sure that many of you reading this book are already aware of the fact that when your clients are invested in the therapy process, their positive outcome potential is greatly enhanced. I have personally recognized among the people whom I have served over my 47-year career that the more deeply invested they are in their program, the more motivated they are going to be to engage in sobriety and abstinence.

Abstinence-mandated therapy goes against that goal of personal investment. When abstinence is mandated, it is normally mandated by a third party. The abstinence, therefore, is not a part of the clients' motivation; it has been imposed on them from another entity or person. They often see it as a form of coercion, and they reject it. When I operationalize abstinence-oriented therapy, I am saying to clients that my hope and goal is for them to achieve abstinence, but I am never going to mandate this as a condition of continued engagement in therapy. Abstinence is the clients' responsibility and privilege to obtain. A question is often asked, however, of how do we proceed when we work in an abstinence-mandated structure? It so happens that many of the people I have seen over the years were brought to me by the Michigan Department of Corrections (MDOC) and, therefore, were mandated in their abstinence. In my contract with the MDOC, my practice did periodic drug screenings. If I had a client who "dropped dirty" during one of the drug screens, I was morally, ethically, and by contract obligated to report that result to the parole agent. The consequence of that finding was entirely up to the parole agent to decide. My focus, however, in my practice was that I was not going to discharge this client because of his dirty drug screen. The reason for that is because we followed the IDDT model of abstinence-oriented therapy; recovery is a process and usually a lifelong process.

This model has several other features that the reader may find of interest. My purpose in recording the features just mentioned was to emphasize what may be the most important element of the relationship you have with people with co-occurring disorders—to continuously provide them with hope. Ken Minkoff calls this the *continuous, hope-providing relationship*.

We accomplish this goal of continuously providing hope to our clients in a variety of different ways. Certainly, being with them during times of slips and relapses gives clients a valuable message of the continuity of our relationship with them. Certainly, refraining from making our relationship with our clients contingent on their sobriety and/ or abstinence is another valuable way of providing them with a sense of hope. I have also found over the years that perhaps the most profoundly impacting method of providing hope to our clients is to consistently be on the lookout for opportunities to affirm their strengths. I can remember many years ago as I was going through my professional education, a very wise professor commented to his class, in regards to providing affirmation statements to our clients, that "nobody is as incompetent as they appear." All clients have strengths. Many of these strengths are well hidden or buried under years of lack of exercise.

Our clients often perform according to their self-confidence. If I am hopeless, I am going to perform in that fashion. If I am hopeful and confident, my actions will reflect that self-perception. Part of our task, at times, is to uncover and/or instill this confidence for our clients. Recall the social experiment that was conducted by Dow Chemical Corporation and the University of Michigan in 2007 that was cited in Chapter 3. Remember the lesson imparted by that event. Our integrated sense of confidence and self-affirmation often determines our competency in task completion.

I have a friend who many years ago achieved an American dream. He was a star athlete in varied sports, but his special love was baseball.

After graduating from high school, he received multiple scholarship offers from various universities. He was also chosen by a major-league baseball team in the annual draft of recent high school and college baseball players. He made a very difficult decision by forgoing the offer from various universities and, instead, joined the organization of the major-league team that drafted him. He began his career at the age of 19 in their low minor-league system. Because of his fascinating love for baseball, he really did not mind the rigors and trials of a minor-league baseball player. In fact, he loved it and actually thrived in this atmosphere. He was a very hard worker and used this time to sharpen his skills. After four years in the minor-league system, he was called up to play at the major-league level. He was thrilled beyond words. He never imagined, as a boy growing up in a small rural community, that he would ever achieve his lifelong dream. But there he was wearing a major-league baseball uniform that was not purchased off the rack of a local sporting goods store, and there he was in a major-league base-ball park and not having to buy a ticket to gain entrance.

His excitement, however, was short-lived. He stayed with the team for 10 games and appeared in four of them. He faced major-league pitching eight times, striking out five times and never registering a hit. After his 10-game experience with this team, he was sent back down to the minor leagues and never again wore the uniform of a major-league baseball team. He toiled in the minor-league system for another four years and eventually decided to leave this dream behind and pursue the rest of his life. He made this decision with grace and pride in what he had accomplished and, as I write this story about him, his life has been very rewarding and he has accomplished much. He is a very dear friend, and many years ago he commented to me that "The challenge is not getting to the major leagues; the challenge is staying in the major leagues." This was a very profound statement from a very wise man.

I am sure that many readers of this book are saddened and dis-tressed when you read data on relapse. Relapse prevention has been a major focus of addictions counseling for decades. This focus deserves all the attention it can get. Although it is certainly not a simple task

165

to move clients into their journey toward sobriety and/or abstinence, it is a significant accomplishment when they stay on that path for the rest of their life. Many of you, I am sure, are fascinated when reading data that reveals that abstinence is achieved as often in people who self-abstained as it is for people who achieve abstinence through counseling. In the realm of people with co-occurring disorders, the data is even more disturbing. Certainly, people with co-occurring disorders are at a significantly elevated vulnerability for relapse. This is why the achievement of moving people with co-occurring disorders onto the path of abstinence and/or sobriety is just the beginning of their journey. It is also the beginning of our journey with them. We are actually very happy that they made it to the major leagues. Now we want them to experience what it is like to stay there.

My fear, however, is that many people who identify themselves as counselors for people with co-occurring disorders actually see their job as merely moving clients toward abstinence. As I mentioned earlier in this book, "all behaviors are purposeful." I have yet to meet an individual in my office who proclaimed to me that his or her goal was to become an addict. Addiction was, perhaps, the farthest thing from these people's minds when they began to use cocaine, heroin, cannabis, or alcohol to provide them with transient relief from life's problems. These people began to use drugs for a reason. That reason was idiosyncratic to the person, but the activity of using drugs became very attractive. It provided them with transient, temporary relief from the symptoms of an emotional, psychological, or psychiatric pain. Their addiction to this drug was a tragic consequence to a behavior that began for a reason. Relapse prevention is focused on the discovery of that goal and providing people with alternative methods of managing that pain other than the use of alcohol and/or drugs. If that is not the focus of relapse prevention work, then we could almost be guaranteed that people with co-occurring disorders will return to drug use. If we do not provide them with other management skills to resolve life's problems, then they will eventually return to their very best friend — drugs. They will do this because they know that drugs will do the job for them.

166

We are, therefore, much more than addictions counselors. This message was given to me very clearly early in my career. It was a message that, as I look back on it, was the watershed event of my career. This framework has allowed me the privilege of having a fairly successful professional career, and it has moved me to recognize that we treat *people* with addiction disorders and not the addiction disorders. Now, let us talk about the varied tasks we have in this endeavor of offering our clients with co-occurring disorders, who are in the early stages of remission, alternative ways to manage life's challenges, so that a return to drug use will be a little less attractive for them.

MINDFULNESS SKILLS

This is the core task. Everything we teach our clients about how to manage life's challenges depends on their becoming mindful. This is an essential task in relapse prevention efforts. In this effort we will be teaching our clients to pay attention to themselves. We want them to be knowledgeable about themselves as people in recovery. We want them to become intimate with their yearnings and their triggers for relapse. We want them to be intimate with their depression, anxiety, dissociative conditions, rage, and all the other psychological and psychiatric entities that moved them to use drugs as a management tool. Why is it essential to teach mindfulness skills to our clients? Because we know that we, as people, generally do not pay attention to our world, and we certainly do not pay attention to ourselves in our world.

You may have heard or read about the social experiment that was organized by the *Washington Post*. In Washington, DC, at a busy Metro station, on a cold January morning in 2007, a man with a violin played six musical arrangements for about one hour. During that one hour, approximately 2,000 people went through the station, most of them on their way to work. After about 10 minutes, a middle-aged man noticed the violinist. He slowed his pace and stopped for a few seconds, and then he hurried on to meet his schedule. A few minutes later, the violinist received his first dollar, as a woman threw money into his hat and without stopping continued to walk. A few minutes after that, a young man leaned against a wall to listen to him, then looked at his watch and started to walk again. A little later on a little boy, estimated at around five years of age, stopped, but his mother tugged him along hurriedly. The little boy stopped to look at the violinist again, but the mother pushed hard and the child continued to walk, turning his head the whole time. This action was repeated by several other children, but every parent, without exception, forced their children to move on quickly. After about 45 minutes, this violinist had played continuously, but only six people had stopped to listen for a short while. About 20 people gave him money, but they continued to walk at their normal pace. The man collected a total of $32 in tips. After one hour, the violinist finished playing and silence took over. No one noticed and no one applauded. There was no recognition at all.

No one knew this, but the violinist was Joshua Bell, one of the most renowned musicians in the world. The music he was playing that morning was one of the most intricate pieces ever written for the violin by Johann Sebastian Bach. The instrument he was playing that morning was a violin worth approximately $3.5 million. That very night, Joshua Bell played in front of a packed audience at the Kennedy Center in Washington, where the seats averaged $200 apiece. That night, in front of that packed audience, they were entertained by Joshua Bell playing the very same music he played that morning at the Metro station during rush hour. The bottom line is that we do not pay attention because we are too busy. Our core task with people with co-occurring disorders in recovery is to teach them skills to slow down and pay attention to their world and themselves in their world.

One of my fondest memories as a young boy was my father's practice of, at least one Sunday per month, taking the family on a car ride. My father would call the ride "taking the scenic route." Basically, the object of the ride was to get lost and to find our way back home. It was my father's job to get us lost, and it was the rest of the family's job to find our way back home. We did this by paying very close attention to all of the markers along the way. Little did my father know, and I doubt this was his goal, but we were being taught mindfulness skills. I continue this tradition today with my children and my grandchildren when, every now and then, we take a ride for the sole purpose of getting lost and finding our way back home. I also call this activity "taking the scenic route." This, in a manner of speaking, is what you want for your clients — encouraging them to "take the scenic route" and pay attention along the way.

I remember several years ago experiencing the gift of one of my more challenging clients discovering his discrepancy. With that discovery, he became motivated to embark on his journey to abstinence. This man was a 49-year-old parolee who had a more than 30-year history of cocaine use. During the initial stages of his counseling with me, during which time he was under court-ordered mandate, he was in significant resistance. His motivation resulted mainly from his discovery that his relationship with his adult daughter was not what he wanted it to be. He also recognized that the difficulty in that relationship was caused by his continuous drug use. He discovered his discrepancy. He was in the early stages of remission, and it was vital that he learned about himself as a person in recovery. It was vital that I engaged in teaching him mindfulness skills.

I said to him, during one of our sessions devoted to mindfulness, "I want you to do something between now and the next time we get together. I want you to take a trip to Grand Rapids and go to the mall. I want you to spend an hour in the mall and be very observant of any act of human kindness that you may see." He reacted to my suggestion with a rather harsh, blunt comment. His comment was intended to inform me that he thought this idea was stupid. I asked him to humor me, and he agreed to pursue this suggestion. The next week I asked him about the results of the trip to the mall. He looked at me and said that he did not see any acts of human kindness, but he did see some "beautiful women." I then asked him what made these women beautiful in his eyes. I began, with a very brief exercise, to initiate him on his journey toward mindfulness. This journey was an absolute essential for him as he became a person in recovery.

STRESS TOLERANCE SKILLS

Our task with our clients is not to eliminate their emotional, psychological, or psychiatric discomfort and pain. Our task is to help them manage this locus of pain and to provide them with alternative management skills that, with appropriate motivation, will replace their maladaptive management styles of drug and/or alcohol use. In Chapter 6 I briefly discussed seeing a 58-year-old woman who, six weeks before I met her, had lost her husband of 34 years. She and her husband were walking out of church on a Sunday morning, and he suddenly collapsed and died from a heart attack. This tragedy occurred one month before his planned retirement. This woman was going through unbearable levels of pain in her grief. She began to manage the pain by drinking significant amounts of wine throughout the day. She was referred to my office by her oldest daughter after she had mentioned to her daughter that she wanted to die.

My therapy goal for this woman was to lead her to a discovery of her discrepancy and, with the resulting motivation to change, teach her mindfulness skills focused on her grief. I wanted her to become quite intimate with her grief, so that she knew what this pain was really about. I then wanted to teach her certain skills that would assist in managing the grief and the pain in ways other than alcohol and thoughts of suicide. The issue, however, was whether she would be a griever for the rest of her life. I cannot, and I should not, embark on a journey where the goal is to eliminate her pain. That is unrealistic and, in many ways, unfair. This woman's lasting memory of her wonderful husband would lie in her grief. I wanted her to experience the grief so she knew this pain eventually dissipates. I also wanted her to know that although the pain does get better, it never goes away, but she can manage it. She can make the unbearable pain bearable pain.

EMOTIONAL REGULATION SKILLS

What skills are we going to teach our clients that will help them manage their emotional, psychological, and psychiatric pain in ways other than through drug and/or alcohol use? We mentioned earlier in this chapter that the role of medication cannot be ignored. Medication designed to alleviate the problematic symptoms of medical mental disorders should be initiated as soon as the dynamics of co-occurring disorders are discovered. Medication should also be in continued use with clients, regardless of the status of their substance use. Medication should be in continuous use because, in no small part, of what Minkoff tells us: "As one problematic issue stabilizes it makes the other issue easier to treat" (Minkoff, 1999).

The focus of this chapter, however, is not on medication. This section is about management skills that we will teach our clients to exercise during times of stress. These behavioral strategies allow clients to feel that they are participants in their own recovery. Although medication is an essential component to the recovery process of people with co-occurring disorders, it is a passive element in treatment. Clients do have to exercise a certain degree of responsibility in taking and managing their medication, but, for the most part, digesting the medication does not give clients the full experience of being in control of their own lives. This issue of control encourages us to teach clients behaviorally focused management skills. These skills are, therefore, designed to give our clients a sense of personal control and management over their pain. In this sense of control there may be a diminished need to turn to drugs for management.

Several years ago I had the privilege and the pleasure of meeting a man who had a significant challenge with rage. According to him, when he became angry, "things got broken and people got hurt." He managed these rage outbursts with the use of cannabis and, periodically, self-mutilation. He came to my office voluntarily and with a major discrepancy in his life that acted as a powerful motivation to change his behaviors. He had fallen in love, and with this feeling came an urge to ask the woman who was the object of his affection to marry him. When he came into my office, he claimed to me that the purpose of his visit was to do something about his rage. He said to me that he wanted to be a good husband and that he wanted to be a better husband to his wife than his father was to his mother. He also indicated that the two of them had been talking about having children. He added that he wanted to be a good father. He wanted to be a better father to his children than his father was to him. This is a powerful discrepancy that led him to be powerfully motivated to change his behaviors. He wanted to explore other ways to manage this rage other than chronic cannabis use and periodic self-mutilation.

The first task with this motivated man was to teach him mindfulness skills. I wanted him to become intimate with his sense of uncontrollable rage and to be alert to the stimulators and the precursors to his rage episodes. I wanted him to be in full recognition of the fact that his cannabis use was a self-medication management style for his rage. I also wanted him to be aware that we could not eliminate his vulnerability to rage episodes. Because of issues from his childhood, he was going to have a psychological vulnerability to temper outbursts for the rest of his life. Our goal was to replace the cannabis use as a management style for his rage with a more adaptive emotional regulation skill.

During one of our sessions, devoted to the emotional regulation component, I suggested a strategy. I suggested that the next time he had a rage experience, he should act in a way opposite to the way he felt. This exercise needed quite a bit of explanation, but he finally agreed to try it after understanding the details of the strategy. This is one of Marsha Linehan's emotional regulation skills that she terms "opposite to emotion" from her *DBT Workbook* (Linehan, 1993).

During his next session, I asked him if he had an opportunity to practice the skill we had discussed the previous week. He indicated to me that he had. As a matter of fact, he indicated that he had a very powerful experience with this newly discovered skill. He then went on to explain his experience: "I'm driving home from work," he explained, "and I'm on the freeway and this moron pulls right in front of me from the entrance ramp. You talk about a rage episode, well, I had the mother lode. I literally wanted to kill him. I was seeing red. I wanted to ram my car into his, push him off the road, and watch his car explode in a ball of flame." I then asked him what he did. He went on to explain, "Well, I have you in my head with this opposite to emotion stuff, so I started singing a song from the *Sound of Music*." And then he started to sing the song. I explained to him that it was not necessary for him to sing the song for me; I just needed to know what happened. He then explained that "it calmed me right down. It was amazing, I've never had anything like this happen to me. I started singing this song and my rage when away. This is weird stuff."

Teaching our clients alternative ways to manage their pain is the heart of the recovery process for people with co-occurring disorders.

EMPATHIC REGARD

People with co-occurring disorders often display the full spectrum of maladaptive behaviors. Many people use alcohol and drugs to reduce painful feelings of self-loathing. Many people use drugs and alcohol to develop the courage to go to work in the morning. They utilize drugs to curb unbearable feelings of rage, depression, anxiety, or psychosis. Whatever dynamics they do bring into our office, we are on a constant watch to never pathologize them. Our clients view their behaviors—maladaptive as they may be—as very beneficial. These behaviors are often seen as very beneficial because they effectively work at curbing and reducing clients' intense levels of discomfort and pain.

One of the early criticisms regarding cognitive-behavioral therapy was that it ran a risk of pathologizing clients. At the very least, it was often seen as lacking in empathy. Many of you who are aware of cognitive-behavioral therapy are aware of the focus on the clients' "irrational core belief system." You are also aware of how the therapist uses a variety of different maneuvers to cognitively rearrange the clients' skewed thinking about themselves or the world in which they live. Although this can be a valuable tool in moving our clients to a more realistic perception of themselves, it can also be misunderstood by our clients as being very unempathic.

How do we exercise empathy in the context of our relationship with people with co-occurring disorders? We are empathic to the clients' view of the benefits of their behavior to manage their unbearable pain. This is not an acceptance, approval, or affirmation of their behaviors; it is merely empathy to the clients' view that their drug and/or alcohol use is, at this time in their lives, seen as helpful. The message we want to give to our clients is that "we get it." We understand the role and function that drugs and alcohol have in their lives at this present time.

If we are lacking in empathy regarding the clients' view of their drug use, we run a significant risk of losing the clients. In many ways this empathic approach is nothing more than a reframe of Miller and Rollnick's strategy in Motivational Interviewing of "rolling with resistance." In Motivational Interviewing, when we roll with clients' resistance, we are accepting the fact that they may have a syntonic view of their behaviors in that they view the behaviors as very helpful, beneficial, and positive. Edwin Shneidman terms this approach as the "empathic regard." He tells us that this is the absolute essential first step in establishing the therapeutic alliance. He tells us that, without this empathic regard, we will never be able to establish the necessary rapport with clients that will move to a positive therapy outcome.

We offer clients alternative ways to manage their pain and discomfort in the context of this empathic regard. We show them other ways to manage their pain as an alternative to drugs and alcohol. Shneidman calls it "removing their blinders" and "expanding their problem-solving options." Drugs and alcohol remain on the table. With appropriate motivation, however, clients may decide to take you up on your offer and decide there is a better way to handle their pain other than drugs.

At a certain point in the therapy relationship, usually after clients have discovered their discrepancy and are willing to engage in the journey to abstinence, I am fond of saying: "I understand your view that alcohol helps manage your grief. Would you like to spend some time with me while we talk about some other ways you can feel management over this pain?" Radical acceptance of clients and the syntonic view of their behavior, while guiding them toward change, is an essential part of therapy for people with co-occurring disorders.

INTERPERSONAL RELATIONSHIP EFFECTIVENESS

It is all about the relationship. It all happens in the room. What we teach, model, and reframe for our clients all happens in the context of our relationship with them. We spoke about this issue extensively in Chapter 3 when we talked about the core task of therapy being the establishment of the therapy relationship.

Many clients use drugs and/or alcohol to enhance their effectiveness in interpersonal functioning. For a variety of reasons, they feel a significant degree of social inadequacy, inhibitions, or absolute fears about interacting with other people. Many clients have, simply stated, poor social skills. Those poor social skills are often demonstrated, ironically, when they are sober and coherent. When they are under the influence of drugs and/or alcohol, however, these social skills may be hidden or go unnoticed. I spoke earlier about the phenomenon of "bonding through Budweiser." Many people develop access to emotions when they are under the influence of drugs and/or alcohol. They become more emotionally intimate during that period of time. Sadly and tragically, when they are sober and alert, they are very closed in an emotional context and, therefore, relationships that demand intimacy are a challenge for them. I recall vividly a scene where the soon-to-be ex-wife of one of my clients, an emergency room doctor, said to me, "the only times in our 20-year marriage that he ever told me he loved me was when he was drunk."

In the context of our therapy relationship, we not only teach new skills, but we also model relationship effectiveness. Recall the young woman I had an opportunity to meet who had been tragically abused as a child. She had served jail time for prostitution, and the prostitution was drug seeking in its goals. She was mandated to addiction counseling to reduce her vulnerability to reengage in prostitution. Her first five sessions were marked by significant rage and anger directed at her therapist—me. She would take any and all opportunities to humiliate me, devalue me, and criticize me. She took great delight in joking about my hairstyle, clothing choice, and posture. Her behavior was understandable; she needed to keep me at a safe distance and operationalize her rage toward men. I could not reveal that insight to her until she was ready to hear it, but I could understand the behavior. Recall that she had been sexually assaulted as a little girl for close to 5 years by three predators in her life—a stepfather, the stepfather's brother, and the stepfather's son. In her view, all men were predators and were scorned. Her condition was complex, but her drug use self-medicated her rage and the issues of her pronounced PTSD. The core task was to develop a relationship.

In one of our early sessions—sixth or seventh, I believe—she was, again, attacking me with a vengeance. During a slight pause in her bombardment, I quietly said to her: "I feel hurt." Her eyes opened wide and she proclaimed: "You're my therapist, you're not sup- posed to say things like that to me!" I replied: "This is a relationship, and this is what we do in relationships." This was the watershed event of her relationship with her therapist. This was, perhaps, the water- shed event in her relational history. She learned in this relationship how to be emotionally available and assertive; how to ask for what she needed; how to be independent and in a relationship; how to establish safe boundaries in a relationship; how to respond to the independence needs of others; how to feel adequate; and how to fall in love and not be hurt or used in that state. I had the privilege of seeing her for close to three years. She discovered a discrepancy when she met a wonder- fully healthy young man; she, therefore, became motivated to pursue abstinence; she learned how to be mindful of herself and her world; she accepted certain stressors as part of her life; she learned how to regulate and manage powerful emotions; she learned how to under- stand herself and self-empathy; and she learned about relationships.

I look back on this young woman now and then. She married that wonderful young man, and they have three healthy boys. I like to think that my intervention—with the steady guidance of my consultant—made a difference in her life. It helps me establish bal- ance when I reflect on my career.

Thank you for reading my book.

—Jack Klott

Co-Occurring Disorders as Factors Associated With Aggressive Behavior

Adolescents exhibit the highest rate of crime and victimization of any age group. The estimated number of violent crimes that are committed at or near schools is 2.7 million per year. Violent crimes perpetrated by adolescents most commonly occur during the hour after school. The rate of violent crimes committed by adolescents is three times higher than the adult rate. Eighty percent of daylight crimes across the United States are perpetrated by out-of-school youth. Seventy-five percent of convicted juvenile offenders are reconvicted between the ages of 17 to 24. Homicide is the leading cause of death among African-American males and the second cause of death among all adolescents.

Several clearly established markers and risk factors indicate vulnerability to aggression among adolescents. The fact that co-occurring disorders begin in adolescence was emphasized in previous chapters. One of the major correlates to violence in the adolescent population is the use of drugs to manage the symptoms of a mental disorder, emotional stressor, or social/environmental disturbance. The importance of diagnosing and treating male and female patients in the realm of co-occurring disorders with gender-specific approaches was also previously addressed. I would, therefore, like to devote some time to capturing, in as concise and organized a fashion as possible, some of the major factors associated with violence in the adolescent population and give these factors a gender-specific approach.

The idea that treatment for girls should be gender specific and that male treatments do not adequately address the unique needs of girls is universally accepted in clinical circles. Also, the pathways to adolescent antisocial and aggressive behaviors are not as clearly understood for girls as they are for boys. Let us then review and consider what we know about the gender differences in antisocial and aggressive behaviors and the function of drug use in these populations.

Incidence of Antisocial and Aggressive Behaviors

1. Boys have higher drug-use patterns than girls and a higher prevalence of violent crimes.
2. In the last 15 years, the rate of girls charged with violent crimes has increased twice as fast as that of boys.
3. Girls are more likely to be incarcerated for minor offenses (e.g., incorrigibility and truancy).
4. Girls represent 26% of total juvenile arrests. Only 1% to 2% of these girls are arrested for violent crimes.
5. An estimated 10% of girls involved in a cross-cultural study achieved the diagnosis of Conduct Disorder as described in the DSM-5 (APA, 2013). Less than 1% received the sociopath specifier (Callous and Unemotional).
6. It appears from studies that female adolescents who are involved in the juvenile justice system are not treated equally to their male counterparts. This system tends to either ignore girls or deal with them more harshly for less serious crimes.
7. Girls who are involved in aggressive behaviors with the added factor of drug use are more likely to be involved in thefts, gang

membership, prostitution, assault, and to be victims of interpersonal violence (IPV).

8. It appears that girls have to reach a higher threshold of deviant behaviors before becoming involved in the Juvenile Justice system.

9. Girls and boys run away from home in about equal numbers. The more sexual abuse the adolescent experiences at home, the more likely he or she is to run away at a younger age.

10. Girls are less likely to be referred to mental health and social services or to educational services than are boys.

Expression of Antisocial and Aggressive Behaviors

1. The specific context in which aggressive/antisocial behavior is expressed and in which it occurs differs for boys versus girls.

2. In the context of relational aggression, girls tend to use more indirect, social, and verbal forms of aggression (and bullying). They tend to harm others in the subtle forms of social exclusion and manipulation, collusion, gossiping, rumor spreading, character defamation, ostracism, and threatening to disclose personal information. Boys in this context use more harsh, direct verbal harassment forms and physical attacks.

3. Girls' aggressive behaviors in a relational context are well thought out and planned. For boys these behaviors are chaotic and impulsive.

4. Females use weapons in personal attacks at a much lower rate than do boys. In the youth category, 96% of assaults that involve a weapon are male correlated.

5. Aggressive and antisocial behaviors among girls result in more severe maladaptive behaviors and outcomes than they do among boys. Girls who are aggressive with physical attacks or who engage in cruel verbal attacks on others (where the intent is to emotionally harm the victim) are more likely to develop traits of the Dyssocial Personality (APA, 2013) and Conduct Disorder with the Callous, Unemotional specifier (APA, 2013). This population is also more vulnerable to acquiring behaviors

179

associated with depression and/or anxiety. They also self-report a higher incidence of loneliness, feelings of abandonment, and rejection. They are also vulnerable to nonsuicidal self-injurious behaviors (APA, 2013) and drug use for the defined purpose of temporary relief from the aforementioned mental and emotional behaviors. In short, they are very vulnerable to becoming the self-medicating population.

6. Females are more likely to direct unregulated anger and rage toward themselves rather than others. As the level of suicide intent increases, so does the frequency of externalized, self-hate behaviors. (See Appendix B, Co-Occurring Disorders as Factors Associated With Suicidal Behaviors.)

Developmental Course of Behaviors

1. Sex role prohibitions against physical aggression are stronger for girls. Physically aggressive girls are more noticeable in a social context and are more disliked by their peers.

2. Be alert to normative cultural roles for females and males as they play out in aggressive behaviors: Boys tend to make up after a fight more quickly than girls do when they fight with other girls; boys who are slighted by other boys have a tendency to shrug it off, whereas girls hold the anger for a much longer period; girls show evidence of more empathy and stronger affiliative tendencies and are more likely to form intimate relationships with a small subset; girls also show more guilt, remorse, and prosocial behaviors, which could provide strengths that are focused for treatment.

3. In adolescents the demonstration of behaviors associated with Conduct Disorder (APA, 2013) and aggression appear to have no gender difference. In elementary school years, the behaviors are profoundly male-gendered.

4. Girls appear to be diagnosed with antisocial and/or conduct disorders later than boys.

5. Girls diagnosed with ADHD (APA, 2013) in elementary school are more likely than boys with ADHD to be diagnosed with Conduct Disorder (APA, 2013).

6. Aggressive girls will have more academic problems and less school connectedness than nonaggressive girls.

7. Aggressive girls engage in relationships with aggressive boys, and this becomes a major correlate to IPV. Girls have been found to bully at a rate of 2.7 episodes per hour, compared to boys who bully at a rate of 5.2 episodes per hour. Bullying behavior in girls toward boys has often been found (20% to 40%) to be attention-seeking in intent and may represent a form of pre-courtship behavior. Bullying for girls in middle school and high school may set them up to select aggressive partners and put themselves at high risk for aggression in relationships (IPV).

8. Suggested remedies to bullying (fighting back and/or ignoring) are both problematic and can make the aggression more physical and harmful to all parties.

9. Girls have a tendency to have more conflicts with parents than do boys. Girls have more problems/conflicts with their fathers than with their mothers.

10. The earlier the age of noted aggressive or antisocial behaviors, the more serious this form of behavior will be in adolescence and adult years. Membership in an aggressive peer group/gang at a young age (10 to 12) will almost always become a correlate to later violent behavior and incarceration in both genders. These issues become, however, intergenerational in females. Girls with Conduct Disorder diagnosis are more likely to have parenting skills deficits and to raise children who will develop aggressive behavioral problems.

11. This developmental pattern in girls with Conduct Disorder (APA, 2013) is further complicated by a higher incidence of psychiatric symptoms, such as depression with suicide activity specifier (APA, 2013), anxiety-driven phobias, obsessive-compulsive personalities, PTSD, eating disorders, and borderline personality disorder.

12. Finally, and most important, this developmental path is exacerbated by the use of substances. The developmental course of substance use appears to be different for boys and girls. Boys tend to associate drug use with pleasurable effects; girls tend to

link drug use with coping strategies and a method of regulating emotions (self-medicating). Girls, therefore, appear to be more vulnerable to using drugs for self-medicating purposes. This frame of self-medicating as a goal of the drug use is powerfully correlated to lower educational attainment, higher vulnerability to drug dependency, higher incidence of being victimized in intimate relationships, early pregnancy and early parenting deficits, higher incidence of poverty, higher vulnerability to loneliness and abandonment, and higher vulnerability to suicide in the female gender.

It is important to mention some evidence-based treatment approaches for this specific population of self-medicators who become involved in violent and aggressive behaviors:

1. On a preventive basis, screen at preschool and early school years for at-risk girls (i.e., girls who are noncompliant, overactive, inattentive, who have difficulty making transitions, difficulty formulating peer relationships, difficulty regulating emotions). Such girls must show evidence of aggressive behavior and engage in high levels of rough play with boys.
2. Provide interventions at the preschool level and engage in ongoing monitoring of such programs in their efforts to help children improve social skills in elementary school and provide children with an opportunity to encounter prosocial peers.
3. Programs modeled after Stop-Now-And-Plan (Earlscourt Child and Family Center, Toronto, Canada, by Kathryn Levene and her colleagues, 1997–2002)
4. Programs recommended by Donald Meichenbaum, PhD, at www.melissainstitute.org
5. Programs recommended by J. Najavits in the Seeking Safety Program at www.seekingsafety.org
6. Programs aimed at bullying issues at www.teachsafeschools.org

REFERENCES FOR APPENDIX A

American Psychiatric Association. (2013). *Diagnostic and statistical manual of mental disorders* (5th ed.; DSM-V). Washington, DC: Author.

Edwards, V. J., Anda, R. F., Dube, S. R., Dong, M., Chapman D. P., & Felitti, V. J. (2005). The wide-ranging health outcomes of adverse childhood experiences. In K. A. Kendall-Tackett & S. M. Giacomoni (Eds.), *Child victimization*. Kingston, NJ: Civic Research Institute.

Liddle, M. D. (2012). Evolutionary theories of violence. *Review of General Psychology, 16*, 24–36.

Tremblay, R. (2010). Developmental origins of disruptive behaviors disorders. *Journal of Childhood Psychology and Psychiatry, 51*, 342–367.

Co-Occurring Disorders as Factors Associated With Suicidal Behavior

In Chapter Six we reviewed some of the elements correlated to risk of completed suicide. One of the major risk factors associated with completed suicide is the existence of co-occurring disorders — people who discover, primarily during adolescence, transient, temporary relief from psychological, psychiatric turmoil when they use drugs. We would like to offer a model for a risk assessment that will, hopefully, be comprehensive yet user-friendly during its operation.

Some Basic Facts About Suicide

1. In any year approximately 30,000 to 35,000 people die from suicide in the United States. This number has a 3% error margin due to misleading nomenclature on death certificates.
2. Of those 30,000 who died from suicide, approximately 5,000 are between the ages of 12 to 19, and 6,000 are female.
3. The number of suicide attempts in any given year is impossible to determine because of subjective descriptors and inaccurate reporting.

4. People who do attempt suicide and are accidentally rescued are at severely increased risk for eventual death by suicide.

5. Suicide is referred to as a very rare event because of the tens of millions of people who carry the significant risk factors of mental disorders, social stressors, and psychological vulnerabilities in any given year.

6. Research on suicide gives us limited information and is based on reviews of small sample populations.

7. There is no causality in suicide. There is no singular, specified factor that leads people to end their existence. Suicide is the ultimate of individual experiences. It results from a complexity of issues pertaining to that person at this time in his or her life. Those issues cause individually defined unbearable pain. For people who cannot cope with this pain, suicide becomes a problem-solving strategy.

8. People who die by suicide rarely communicate their suicide intent right before the tragic event. Those who do not communicate have a higher incidence of drugs being used for self-medicating purposes.

9. Adolescents (12 to 19) rarely leave suicide notes.

10. Females attempt suicide at a greater rate than do men, but men die by suicide at a greater rate than do women, because men use more lethal means when they attempt to end their lives.

11. Gay, lesbian, bisexual, and transgendered adolescents have an elevated risk for suicide when they are rejected and/or bullied as they acknowledge their sexual orientation.

12. Adolescents are at an elevated risk for suicide when their families relocate and this relocation results in conflicts with family, termination of important relationships, acculturation challenges, loneliness, victimization by bullying, loss of peer status, or loss of autonomy. There is no correlation between adolescent suicide and the isolated issue of family relocation.

13. Suicide rates among Native American Indians vary greatly among tribal groups.

14. An estimated 90% to 97% of people who died from suicide and were studied had a mental disorder at the time of their death.

15. Of those with a mental disorder at the time of death, 70% had a depressive disorder compounded by a drug-use disorder, and the purpose of the drug use was to self-medicate.
16. Suicide has been, and continues to be, a Caucasian issue.
17. Men and women who lose a loved one to suicide (survivors of suicide) can experience a life-threatening form of grieving termed the Bereavement Disorder (APA, 2013).
18. Having a sense of being loved, having access to one's emotions, and feeling safe from harm in the current social environment are all seen as protective factors from suicide.
19. Being introduced to medications for the relief of depression and achieving that goal does not act as a protective factor from suicide.
20. There is no correlation between inpatient psychiatric placement and protective factors from suicide.

RISK ASSESSMENTS FOR SUICIDE INTENT

Avoid using standardized risk assessments as a stand-alone evaluation. They do not protect in litigation, and there are no suicide predictor scales. Instead, we are urged to use a risk assessment format that actually has a focus on the risk factors for suicide, for example:

1. Examine possible dysthymia conditions (chronic depression) when the client is self-medicating the issue with alcohol.
2. Examine possible major depression episodes, especially single episodes with psychotic features. In females, remain alert for major depression with postpartum onset.
3. Examine possible bipolar II conditions, especially during the hypomanic phase with a noted increase in irritable mood. Also, remain alert to the bipolar I disorder where the clients caused significant disruption in their lives during their manic phase.
4. Examine possible chronic symptoms of PTSD that are included in the expanded diagnosis in the DSM-5 (APA, 2013). Remain alert to clients who are self-medicating with cannabis and/or alcohol and the severity of depression in the display of symptoms.

5. Examine for possible generalized anxiety disorder where the person is self-medicating with cannabis.

6. Examine the psychotic disorder of schizophrenia, especially when the client expresses hopelessness about the course of the disorder and the effect of the disorder on their goals, dreams, and aspirations. Examine any integrated depressive or anxiety symptoms with the psychotic symptoms.

7. Examine the role of drug/alcohol use for self-medicating purposes.

8. Examine with the client any issues of:
   Health concerns
   Aloneness, rejection, abandonment
   Financial concerns
   Loss of occupational definition
   Loss of autonomy
   Loss of social definition
   Performance anxiety
   Emotional constriction
   Hopelessness
   Severe self-devaluation
   Family discord and pathology
   Easy access to firearms

9. Examine the client for any behaviors considered to indicate immediate risk:
   Display of psychological turmoil
   Change in eating/sleeping habits
   Increase in irritation
   Comments of hopelessness and helplessness
   Evaluate for history of valid suicide attempts
   Anhedonia
   Dysphoria
   Morbid preoccupation with the past
   Talks about specific planning
   Talks about apathy toward life and an anticipation of death
   No capacity for future thoughts
   Rapid change from turmoil to peacefulness

Denies suicide intent

Denies having any problems

Denies needing to talk to anyone

10. Also evaluate for protector factors:

Not wanting to hurt loved ones

Appropriate reasons for living

Demonstrated ambivalence toward suicide

Spiritual issues

Healthy support system

11. Pay very close attention to specificity of planning and rapid change of behavior from psychological turmoil to peace and calm, which may be an indication that the plan and wish to die is complete.

12. Assessments must always be done in the context of a clinical interview. If a standardized assessment is used, the function of that measurement is to validate the material discovered during the clinical interview.

13. Avoid the use of the No Suicide Contract format. These methods do not work, and they do not protect the therapist from litigation.

14. Based on the level of concern, discuss and document levels of intervention and follow-up care plans.

REFERENCES FOR APPENDIX B

Klott, J. (2004). *The suicide and homicide risk assessment and treatment planner*. Hoboken, NJ: Wiley.

Klott, J. (2012). *Suicide and psychological pain: Assessments and treatment*. Eau Claire, WI: Premier.

References

American Psychiatric Association. (2000). *Diagnostic and statistical manual of mental disorders* (4th ed., text rev.; DSM-IV-TR). Washington, DC: Author.

American Psychiatric Association. (2013). *Diagnostic and statistical manual of mental disorders* (5th ed.; DSM-V). Washington, DC: Author.

Ashley, O. S., Marsden, M. E., & Brady, T. M. (2003). Effectiveness of substance abuse treatment programming for women: A review. *American Journal of Drug and Alcohol Abuse, 29*, 19–53.

Bartels, S. J., & Thomas, W. N. (1991). Lessons from a pilot residential program for people with dual diagnoses of SPMI and SA. *Psychosocial Rehabilitation Journal, 15*, 19–30.

Beck, A., Wright, F., Newman, C., & Liese, B. (1993). *Cognitive therapy of substance abuse*. New York, NY: Guilford Press.

Bernstein, D. P., Stein, J. A., Newcomb, M. D., Walker, E., Pogge, D., Ahluvalia, T., . . . Zule, W. (2003). Development and validation of a brief screening version of the childhood trauma questionnaire. *Child Abuse & Neglect, 27*(2), 169–190. doi: 10.1016/S0145-2134(02)00541-0

Bowlby, J. (1969). Disruption of affectional bonds and its effects on behavior. *Canada's Mental Health Supplement, 59*, 12–12.

Bowlby, J. (1982). *Attachment* (2nd ed.). New York, NY: Basic Books.

Bowlby, J. (1988). *A Secure Base*. New York, NY: Basic Books.

Chapman, A. L., Specht, M. W., & Cellucci, T. (2005). Factors associated with suicide attempts in female inmates: The hegemony of hopelessness. *Suicide & Life - Threatening Behavior, 35*(5), 558–69.

Clark, D. (1988, April). *Epidemiology of suicide.* Keynote address at the Annual Conference of the American Association of Suicidology, Washington D.C.

Clark, D. C. (1993). Narcissistic crisis of aging and social despair. *Suicide & Life Threatening Behavior, 23,* 21–26.

Clark, D. C., & Fawcett, J. A. (1992a). An empirically based model of suicide risk assessment with affective disorders. In D. G. Jacobs (Ed.), *Suicide and clinical practice* (pp. 55–73). Washington, DC: American Psychiatric Press.

Clark, D. C., & Fawcett, J. A. (1992b). Review of empirical risk factors in the suicidal patient. In B. Bongard (Ed.), *Suicide: Guidelines for assessment, management, and treatment* (pp. 16–48). New York, NY: Oxford University Press.

Coffey, S. F., Brady, K. T., & Bock, S. E. (2004). Substance abuse and posttraumatic stress disorder. *Current Directions in Psychological Science, 13,* 206–209.

Cornelius, J. R., Salloum, I. M., & Mezzich, J. (1995). Suicidality in patients with comorbid major depression and alcoholism. *American Journal of Psychiatry, 152,* 358–364.

Daly, D. C., & Salloum, I. (1991). Integrated dual disorders program in an acute care psychiatric program hospital. *Professional Review Journal, 15,* 45–56.

Dozier, M., & Tyrrell, C. (1998). The role of attachment in therapeutic relationships. In J. A. Simpson & W. S. Rholes (Eds.), *Attachment theory and close relationships* (pp. 221–248). New York, NY: Guilford Press.

Drake, R. E., Mercer, C., Mueser, K., McHugo, G. J., & Bond, G. R. (1999). Review of integrated mental health and substance abuse treatment for patients with severe mental illness: A review of recent research. *Schizophrenia Bulletin, 24,* 589–608.

Dunner, D. L., Gershon, E. S., & Godwin, F. K. (1976). Heritable factors in the severity of affective illness. *Biology of Psychiatry, 11,* 31–42.

Fallot, R. D., & Harris, M. (2002). The trauma recovery and empowerment model (TREM): Conceptual and practical issues in a group intervention for women. *Community Mental Health Journal, 38*(6), 475–485. doi: 10.1023/A:1020880101769

Farber, B. A., & Metzger, J. A. (2009). The therapist as secure base. In *Attachment theory and research in clinical work with adults.* (pp. 46–70). New York, NY, US: Guilford Press, New York, NY.

Farber, L. H. (1962). Despair and the life of suicide. *Existential Psychological Psychiatry, 2,* 125–139.

Feeney, N. C., Foa, E. B., Treadwell, K. R. H., & March, J. (2004). Posttraumatic stress disorder in youth: A critical review of the cognitive and behavioral treatment outcome literature. *Professional Psychology: Research and Practice, 35,* 466–476.

Ford, J. D., Gelernter, J., DeVoe, J. S., Zhang, W., & Weiss, R. D. (2009). Association of psychiatric and substance abuse disorders comorbidity with cocaine dependence severity and treatment utilization in cocaine dependent individuals. *Drug and Alcohol Dependence, 99,* 193–203.

Gange, S. J., Barrón, Y., Greenblatt, R. M., Anastos, K., Minkoff, H., Young, M., . . . Muñoz, A. (2002). Effectiveness of highly active antiretroviral therapy among HIV-1 infected women. *Journal of Epidemiology and Community Health, 56*(2), 153–159. doi: http://dx.doi.org/10.1136/jech.56.2.153

Greenfield, S. F., & Pirard, S. (2009). *Gender-specific treatment for women with substance use disorders.* New York, NY, US: Guilford Press, New York, NY.

Greenfield, S. F., Weiss, R. D., Muenz, L. R., Vagge, L. M., Kelly, J. F., Bello, L. R., & Michael, J. (1998). The effect of depression on return to drinking: A prospective study. *Archives of General Psychiatry, 55*(3), 259–265. doi: 10.1001/archpsyc.55.3.259

Grella, C. E. (2009). Treatment seeking and utilization among women with substance abuse disorders. In C. E. Grella (Ed.), *Women and addiction: A comprehensive handbook* (pp. 307–322). New York, NY: Guilford Press.

Grencavage, M., & Norcross, J. (1990). Where are the commonalities among the therapeutic common factors? *Professional Psychology: Research and Practice, 21,* 372–378.

Handmaker, N. S., Packard, W. R., & Conforti, M. (2002). Findings of a pilot study of motivational interviewing with pregnant drinkers. *Journal of Studies on Alcohol, 60,* 285–287.

Heather, N., Rollnick, S., & Bell, A. (1992). Predictive validity of the readiness to change questionnaire. *Addiction, 88*, 1667–1677.

Heather, N., Rollnick, S., & Bell, A. (1996). Effects of brief counseling among male heavy drinkers identified on general hospital wards. *Drug and Alcohol Review, 15*, 29–38.

Heather, N., Rollnick, S., Bell, A., & Richmond, R. (1996). Effects of brief counselling among male heavy drinkers identified on general hospital wards. *Drug and Alcohol Review, 15*(1), 29–38. doi:http://dx.doi.org/10.1080/09595239600185641

Hien, D., Litt, L. C., Cohen, L. R., Miele, G. M., & Campbell, A. (2009). Perspectives on traumatic stress, posttraumatic stress disorder, and complex posttraumatic stress disorder. *Trauma services for women in substance abuse treatment: An integrated approach* (pp. 9–17). Washington, DC: American Psychological Association. doi: 10.1037/11864-001

Jacobs, D. G., & Brown, H. N. (1989). *Suicide: Understanding and responding.* Madison, CT: International University Press.

Jamison, K. (1995). *An unquiet mind: A memoir of moods and madness.* New York, NY: Knopf.

Jerrell, J. M., & Ridgely, M. S. (1995). Comparative effectiveness of three approaches to serving people with severe mental illness and substance abuse disorders. *Journal of Nervous and Mental Disease, 183*, 566–576.

Kelly, M. J. (1999). Medical settings and suicide. In R. Maris (Ed.), *Suicide assessment and intervention* (pp. 491–501). San Francisco, CA: Jossey-Bass.

Klerman, G. L. (1987). Clinical epidemiology of suicide. *Journal of Clinical Psychiatry, 48*, 33–38.

Klott, J., & Jongsma, A. E. (2006). *The co-occurring treatment planner.* Hoboken, NJ: Wiley.

Linehan, M. M. (1993). *Cognitive-behavioral treatment of borderline personality disorder.* New York, NY, US: Guilford Press, New York, NY.

Linehan, M. M. (1999). *Standard protocol for assessing and treating suicidal behaviors for patients in treatment.* San Francisco, CA, US: Jossey-Bass, San Francisco, CA.

Linehan, M. M., Armstrong, H. E., Suarez, A., & Allmon, D. (1991). Cognitive-behavioral treatment of chronically parasuicidal

References

borderline patients. *Archives of General Psychiatry, 48*(12), 1060–1064. doi: 10.1001/archpsyc.1991.01810360024003

Linehan, M. M., Dimeff, L. A., Reynolds, S. K., Comtois, K. A., Welch, S. S., Heagerty, P., & Kivlahan, D. R. (2002). Dialectical behavior therapy versus comprehensive validation therapy plus 12-step for the treatment of opioid dependent women meeting criteria for borderline personality disorder. *Drug and Alcohol Dependence, 67*(1), 13–26. doi: http://dx.doi.org/10.1016/S03768716(02)00011-X

Maris, R. W. (1992). *Assessment and predication of suicide.* New York, NY: Guilford Press.

Maris, R. W. (1992). How are suicides different? In *Assessment and prediction of suicide.* (pp. 65–87). New York, NY, US: Guilford Press, New York, NY.

Maris, R. W. (1998). *Pathways to suicide: A survey of self-destructive behaviors.* Baltimore, MD: Johns Hopkins University Press.

McMain, S., Sayrs, J. H. R., Dimeff, L. A., & Linehan, M. M. (2007). Dialectical behavior therapy for individuals with borderline personality disorder and substance dependence. (pp. 145–173). New York, NY, US: Guilford Press, New York, NY.

Meichenbaum, D. (2009). Core psychotherapeutic tasks with returning soldiers: A case conceptualization approach. In S. Morgillo-Freeman, B. A. Moore, & A. Freeman (Eds.), *Living and surviving in harm's way* (pp. 193–210). New York, NY: Routledge.

Meichenbaum, D. (2010). Effective treatment for the self-medicating mentally ill. Presentation at The New England Educational Institute Conference, Eastham, MA, August, 19, 2010.

Miller, W. R., Benefield, R. G., & Tonigan, J. S. (1998). Enhancing motivation for change in problem drinking: A controlled comparison of two therapist styles. *The Journal of Consulting and Clinical Psychology, 61,* 455–461.

Miller, W. R., & Rollnick, S. (2002). *Motivational Interviewing: Preparing people for change.* New York, NY: Guilford Press.

Minkoff, K. (1989). Development of an integrated model for the treatment of patients with dual diagnosis of psychosis and addiction. *Hospital Community Psychiatry, 40,* 1031–1036.

Minkoff, K. (1993). Intervention strategies for people with dual diagnosis. *Innovations & Research, 2*, 11–17.

Minkoff, K. (1994). Models for addictions treatment in psychiatric populations. *Psychiatric Annals, 24*, 412–417.

Minkoff, K. (2001). Developing standards of care for individuals with co-occurring psychiatric and substance use disorders. *Psychiatric Services, 52*(5), 597–599. doi: http://dx.doi.org/10.1176/appi.ps.52.5.597

Minkoff, K., & Cline, C. A. (2004). Changing the world: The design and implementation of comprehensive continuous integrated systems of care for individuals with co-occurring disorders. *Psychiatric Clinics of North America, 27*(4), 727–743. doi: http://dx.doi.org/10.1016/j.psc.2004.07.003

Minkoff, K., & Regner, J. (1999). Innovations in integrated dual diagnosis treatment in public managed care: The choate dual diagnosis case rate program. *Journal of Psychoactive Drugs, 31*(1), 3–12. doi: 10.1080/02791072.1999.10471720

Moscicki, E. K. (1997). Identification of suicide risk factors. *Psychiatric Clinician of North America, 20*, 499–517.

Motto, J. A. (1985). Paradoxes of suicide risk assessment. *Journal of Clinical Psychiatry, 7*, 109–119.

Mueser, K. T., Noordsy, D. L., Drake, R. E., & Fox, L. (2003). In Barlow D. H. (Ed.), *Integrated treatment for dual disorders: A guide to effective practice*. New York, NY: Guilford Press.

Murphy, E., Smith, R., Lindesay, J., & Slattery, J. (1988). Increased mortality rates in late life depression. *British Journal of Psychiatry, 152*, 347–353.

Najavits, L. M. (2006). Seeking safety: Therapy for posttraumatic stress disorder and substance use disorder. (pp. 228–257). New York, NY, US: Guilford Press, New York, NY

Najavits, L. M., Sonn, J., Walsh, M., & Weiss, R. D. (2004). Domestic violence in women with PTSD and substance abuse. *Addiction Behavior, 29*, 707–715.

Najavits, L. M., Weiss, R. D., & Shaw, R. (1997). The link between substance abuse and PTSD in women. *American Journal on Addictions, 6*, 273–283.

References

Newman, S. C., & Thompson, A. H. (2003). A population-based study of the association between pathological gambling and attempted suicide. *Suicide & Life Threatening Behavior, 33*, 80–87.

Peele, S. (1989). *Diseasing of America: Addiction treatment out of control.* Lexington, MA: Heath.

Prochaska, J. O., & DiClemente, C. C. (1986). Toward a comprehensive model of change. *Treating Addiction Behaviors, 3*, 3–27.

Prochaska, J. O., DiClemente, C. C., & Norcross, J. C. (1992). In search of how people change: Applications to addictive behaviors. *American Psychologist, 47*(9), 1102–1114. doi:http://dx.doi.org/10.1037/0003-066X.47.9.1102

Regier, D. A., Farmer, M. A., Rae, D. P., Locke, B. Z., Keith, S. J., Judd, L. L., & Goodwin, F. K. (1992). Comorbidity of mental disorders with alcohol and other drug abuse. *Journal of the American Medical Association, 264*, 2511–2518.

Rihmer, Z. (1990). Suicide in subtypes of primary major depression. *Journal of Affective Disorders, 20*, 87–91.

Roberts, M. (1997). *The man who listens to horses.* New York, NY: Random House.

Roy, A., & Draper, R. (1995). Suicide among psychiatric hospital patients. *Psychological Medicine, 25*, 199–202.

Roy, A., & Linnoila, M. (1990). Monoamines and suicidal behavior. In *Violence and suicidality: Perspectives in clinical and psychobiological research.* (pp. 141–183). Philadelphia, PA, US: Brunner/Mazel, Philadelphia, PA. Retrieved from http://search.proquest.com/docview/617862502?accountid=15099

Sabbath, J. C. (1969). The suicidal adolescent: The expendable child. *Journal of the American Academy of Child and Adolescent Psychiatry, 8*, 272–279.

Saxon, S. (1980). Self-destructive behavior patterns in male and female drug abusers. *American Journal of Drug Abuse, 7*, 19–29.

Schneidman, E. (1971, April). *Psych Ache.* Keynote address at the Annual Conference of the American Association of Suicidology, Toronto, Canada.

Shiffman, S. (1982). Relapse following smoking cessation: A situational analysis. *Journal of Consulting and Clinical Psychology, 50*, 71–86.

Shneidman, E. S. (1973). Suicide notes reconsidered. *Psychiatry: Journal for the Study of Interpersonal Processes, 36*(4), 379–394.

Shneidman, E. S. (1985). *Definition of suicide.* New York, NY: Wiley.

Shneidman, E. S. (1993). Suicide as psyche ache. *Journal of Nervous Mental Disorders, 181,* 147–149.

Shneidman, E. S. (1994). Clues to suicide reconsidered. *Suicide & Life Threatening Behaviors, 24,* 395–397.

Sinha, R., & Rounsaville, B. J. (2002). Sex-depressed substance abusers. *Journal of Clinical Psychiatry, 63,* 616–627.

Stalone, F. (1990). Statistical predictors of suicide in depressives. *Comprehensive Psychiatry, 21,* 381–387.

Stimmel, B. (1991). *The facts about drug use: Coping with drugs and alcohol in your family, at work, in your community.* New York, NY: Consumer Reports Books.

Sullivan, H. S. (1954). *Conceptions of modern psychiatry.* Oxford, England: William Alanson White Psychiatric.

The New Hampshire-Dartmouth Integrated Dual Disorder Treatment Model (2002). Case Western Reserve University, Cleveland, Ohio. Retrieved from http://www.ohiosamiccoe.case.edu.

Velasquez, M. M., Carbonari, J. P., & DiClemente, C. C. (1999). Psychiatric severity and behavior change in alcoholism. *Addictive Behaviors, 24,* 481–496.

Washington, G (2007). Pearls before breakfast: Can one of the nation's great musicians cut through the fog of a D.C. rush hour? Let's find out. *The Washington Post.* Retrieved from: http://www.washingtonpost.com/wp-dyn/content/article/2007/04/04/AR2007040401721.html

Weiner, H., & Fox, S. (1982). Cognitive–behavioral therapy with substance abusers. *Social Casework, 63*(9), 564-567. Retrieved from http://search.proquest.com/docview/616750344?accountid=15099

Whiston, S., & Sexton, T. (1993). An overview of psychotherapy outcome research. *Professional Psychology: Research and Practice, 24,* 43–51.

Zuckoff, A., & Daly, D. C. (1999). Dropout prevention and dual diagnoses clients. *The Counselor, 2,* 23–27.

About the Author

Jack Klott has recently retired from a 40-year career as a counselor for people with mental disorders and substance use disorders. He is the author of the *Suicide and Homicide Risk Assessment and Treatment Planner* (Wiley, 2004), the *Co-occurring Disorders Treatment Planner* (Wiley, 2006), and *Suicide and Psychological Pain* (Premier Publishing, 2012). He currently is a national speaker on the topics of suicide, motivational interviewing, co-occurring disorders, and the DSM. He is a founder of the Michigan Association of Suicide Prevention, an organization that recently honored him for his contribution to suicide prevention in that state. He can be reached at jackklott@aol.com.

Author Index

AUTHOR INDEX

Meichenbaum, D., 4, 5, 6, 14, 15, 16, 28, 48, 50, 51, 58, 59–60, 66, 67, 80, 86, 108, 127, 152, 155, 160
Mercer, C., 86
Mezzich, J., 127
Miele, G. M., 15
Miller, W. R., 7, 8, 11, 69, 79, 80, 83, 87, 89, 99, 160, 174
Minkoff, K., 4, 6, 12–13, 16–17, 58, 71, 80, 86, 122–123, 127, 151, 158, 159, 162, 163, 164, 171
Moscicki, E. K., 134
Motto, J. A., 145
Mueser, K. T., 15, 86

Najavits, L. M., 16
Newman, C., 57
Newman, S. C., 36
Noordsy, D. L., 15
Norcross, J., 58, 60, 80, 124, 160

Ohio SAMI CCOE, 159

Packard, W. R., 86
Peele, S., 24
Prochaska, J. O., 58, 60, 80, 160

Regier, D. A., 13, 30, 127
Ridgely, M. S., 85
Rihmer, Z., 45

Roberts, M., 73
Rollnick, S., 7, 8, 11, 69, 79, 80, 83, 87, 89, 99, 160, 174
Rounsaville, B. J., 19

Sabbath, J. C., 55, 118, 133
Salloum, I. M., 127
Saxon, S., 37
Sexton, T., 124
Shiffman, S., 106
Shneidman, E. S., 9, 90, 125, 126, 130, 133, 134, 135, 145, 174
Sinha, R., 19
Stalone, F., 45
Stimmel, B., 24
Suarez, A., 132
Sullivan, H. S., 12, 38–39, 58, 69, 70–71, 108

Thompson, A. H., 36
Tonigan, J. S., 83
Tyrrell, C., 70

Velasquez, M. M., 101

Weiss, R. D., 15
Whiston, S., 124
Wright, F., 57

Zhang, W., 15
Zuckoff, A., 35

202

Subject Index

203

Subject Index

Juvenile Justice system, 178, 179

Legal system:
  legal guardian and, 155
  legal problems, 118
  therapy ordered through, 10, 57
  violent behavior and, 110
Life expectations, 74–75, 81
Life views, childhood, 76
Listening to client, 65, 90, 103, 127. *See also*
  Empathic attitude
Living alone, 13
Long-term goals, 114–121
Love, security and, 129–130
Low energy levels, 34
Low self-esteem, 34, 52, 112

Maintaining factors, 108–110
Major depression. *See also* Depressive disorder
  co-occurring substance-related disorder
    and, 13
  drugs and alcohol for, 37
  high mortality and, 36–37
  as predisposing factor, 34–35
Major mental disorders:
  emergence of symptoms and, 22
  suicide and, 127
Maladaptive behaviors:
  case conceptualization and, 108–110
  purposeful behaviors and, 104
Maladaptive coping mechanisms, 22, 41, 56, 170
Mandated reporting, 72
Mandated treatment:
  assertion of autonomy and, 110–111
  DUI and, 114
  highly at-risk clients and, 83
  mandated clients, 57–58
  motivation and, 87, 119
  outcomes and, 59–60
  resistance to, 57–58, 71, 72
The Man Who Listens to Horses (Roberts), 73
Marital problems, 27, 142, 144
MDOC. *See* Michigan Department of
  Corrections (MDOC)
Medical care, 144
Medical conditions:
  general, 49–50
  serious, suicide risk and, 13
Medication. *See also* Prescription drugs
  as adaptive coping mechanism, 22
  antidepressant, 139
  mood-stabilizing, 46
  noncompliance and, 157
  pain, 37

Men:
  co-occurance and, 13
  male therapist, 71
  suicide completion and, 138, 142, 146
Mental disorder. *See also* Mental illness
  definition, 22
  emerging symptoms of, 23, 24
  substance use and, 142
  treatment strategies and, 158
Mental health care:
  addiction and (*see* Addiction counseling)
  agencies, 18
  integrated programs, 86–87
  program coordination and, 85–86
Mental illness. *See also* Dysthymia; Mental
  disorder; specific disorder
  decompensation and, 158
  emerging symptoms of, 22
  relapse and, 105
  self-medication and, 4, 71
  severity of (*see* Quadrants, case
    conceptualization and)
  substance-related disorders and, 13
  undiagnosed, untreated, 4
Mental status exam, 143, 148
Metabolic conditions, 49
Methadone clinics, 161
Methamphetamine, 37, 45
Method of dialogue, 73
Michigan Department of Corrections
  (MDOC), 163
Mindfulness skills, 167–169
Mini-mental status exam, 51
Modeling, parental, 109
Mood disorders:
  anxiety disorder and, 21
  general medical conditions and,
    49–50
  substance-induced, 6
Mood-stabilizing medication, 46
"Mood swings," 46
Morphine, 50
Motivation. *See also* Adaptations of
  motivational interviewing
  behavior change and, 12, 112
  effective treatment and, 158
  integrated programs and, 87–90
  lack of, 157
  mindfulness and, 169
  monitoring of, 158
  parental relationship and, 98, 103
Motivational Enhancement Therapy
  seminar, 2
Motivational interviewing, 69

Subject Index

213

Suicide risk assessment:
first task in, 125–126
populations and (*see* Suicidal populations)
predictions for persons at risk, 145–150
psychological vulnerabilities (*see*
Psychological vulnerabilities)
risk factors, 126, 187–189
Support groups, 146–147, 156
Survival instinct, 139
Survivors of Suicide support group, 146–147
Symptom management, 22
Syntonic presentation, 54, 75

"Taking the scenic route," 168–169
Tattoos, multiple, 51
Termination of therapy, 80
Therapist "in recovery," 78
Therapy:
client seeking (*see* Reasons for seeking
therapy)
lack of, 146
as process, not event, 124
reciprocal/mutual relationship, 112
resistance to (*see* Resistance to therapy)
termination of, 80
three essentials in, 17
treatment plans, 114
Therapy alliance:
angry clients and, 79
arguments and, 65
beginning of process, 59, 69 (*see also* Case
conceptualization)
confrontations and, 67
"core task," development of, 57
first step in establishing, 174
implications for, determining, 121
outcomes and (*see* Treatment outcomes)
strengths of clients and, 111–112
Therapy relationship:
context of, therapy and, 71–72
flexibility in, 99
goals in (*see* Goals in therapy relationship)
individualized (*see* Individualized therapy)
integrated strategies and, 17
mutual, therapy and, 90
successful therapy experience and, 124
Third parties, 72
"Tired feelings," 23, 26
Transference, 70
Trauma, intense. *See also specific type*
childhood, 39, 67
defense mechanisms and, 58

large-scale events and, 16
multiple exposures, 15
professions and, 132
psychosocial stressors and, 22
substance use disorders and, 14
women and, 18
Trauma-specific interventions, 17
Treatment compliance, 14
Treatment history, 119
Treatment outcomes:
case conceptualization and, 124
client alcohol use and, 13
confidence in ability to change and, 80
early detection and, 25
failures, multiple, 128
Treatment plans, 114
Trust, 74
TRV (Technical Rules Violation
Center for violators of stipulations
of parole), 82

Unemployment, 13, 26, 118
University of Michigan, 74–75, 164
Urinary tract infection, 49

Veterans Administration, 2, 155
Victimization incidents, 15
Violence. *See also* Aggressive behavior; Child
abuse; Domestic violence; Physical
abuse; Suicide
aggression through modeling, 109–110
fear of change and, 74
hostility and, 79
interpersonal (IPV), 179, 181
Voluntary counseling, 60

Walter, story of, 58–59
Washington Post, 167
Watershed event, 103, 167, 176
Wayne State University, 74–75
Welcoming attitude, 72
The Wind in the Willows (Grahame), 88
Wisdom, 23, 70, 108, 112
Withdrawal symptoms, 128
Women:
addiction counseling settings and, 18
female therapist, 72
gender differences and, 17–19
suicide attempts and, 138
Worldview of client, 118
Worthlessness, feelings of, 93,
109, 134